Success with
Plants for your
Garden Pond

D0520281

ANTJE JANSEN

Series Editor
LESLEY YOUNG

MEREHURST

Introduction

Contents

Plants are the living soul of a garden pond. They endow the pond with life as well as beauty for they play an important role in the well-being of the fauna of the pond. The right kind of planting will turn your garden pond into a small natural habitat – the secret aim of many pond owners. Of course, an essential prerequisite for this is to get to know as much as you can about the art of water gardening. The path to success begins with your choice of plants. This guide provides precise instructions for the correct planting of marginal areas and shallow and deep water zones. Lovely colour photographs and detailed advice on the care of many of the most beautiful water plants for either an ornamental or wild pond will help you to realize your ambition. The practical sections contain explicit illustrations and detailed instructions for planting, care and propagating. In addition, there are special tips, e.g. how to care for water-lilies, how to over-winter more sensitive pond plants, which plants are suitable for a shaded pond, and how to improve conditions in the pond to help your plants to thrive.

There are plenty of examples of planting in different zones of the garden pond, using baskets, plant containers, verge matting and plant islands, thus making it easy to equip a pond with plants that are full of flower from spring to autumn.

Mimulus 'Roter Kaiser'.

Iris orientalis.

Sunbathing frog.

The author

Biologist Antje Jansen lectures on garden pond design and pond building. Since 1988 she has been engaged in scientific research on the nutrient supply of plant communities.

NB: Please read through the Author's note on page 63 so that your enjoyment of your garden pond may remain unimpaired.

Plants are the soul of a garden pond

Healthy pond plants not only make a pond more beautiful, they are also very important because a garden pond cannot function properly without plants. In addition, such a pond will provide a habitat for much fascinating wildlife, which will gradually appear as visitors or residents in and around your pond.

If you set out to establish a garden pond with a great variety of healthy plantlife and a large range of pond creatures, you will be providing for your own pleasure as well as creating a never-ending source of interest for your children and a means of having the magic of nature within your own garden. When designing and building your garden pond, and later on too, correct planting will ensure that many water beetles, dragonflies, frogs and other pond fauna take up residence in your garden pond. For example, tall clumps of reeds will provide a refuge for creatures that require a hiding place. Creatures that like a sunny environment will need areas with low-growing plants. Correct planting will also help to provide good-quality water.

A plant-friendly design for a garden pond
Even in the early stages of designing your pond, you can make sure that a great variety of water and marginal plants will flourish. The most important criteria for the well-

being of all pond plants are the position of the pond, the ground underneath it and the quality of the water in the pond.
The various vitally different areas within a pond – the different zones (illustration, p. 6) – can be achieved quite easily through creating various angles of slope of the bank and different depths of water in the pond. A range of different zones will ensure that you can introduce a variety of plant species.
NB: You will find tips on the design of a plant-friendly garden pond in the following pages. For those readers who already have a garden pond that may not yet be quite suitable for plants, there are a number of simple improvements on pages 8 and 9.

Tips on the positioning of a pond
Light is absolutely essential for the growth of all pond plants. One basic rule applies: the more daylight a plant receives under adequate conditions of nutrient supply, oxygen content of water and water

temperature, the better it will grow. Obviously, however, when choosing a position for a plant, the light requirements of that particular plant still have to be considered.
Sun: Sunlight all day long is not absolutely necessary for a garden pond but a minimum of five hours of sunlight per day is considered to be crucial for many plants.
Shade: If a sunny position is not available, you can equally well design a shady pond with plants that like shade (see p. 17). This means that you will not enjoy as many flowers as you would do if you created a sunny pond. You will also have to plan the design much more carefully in order to use the available light to the best advantage.
Be careful under trees: When choosing a position for the pond, much can be done to ensure good-quality water in the long term. In general, avoid a position under trees, to prevent the water from becoming polluted by falling seeds or leaves.

Size and depth
Any body of water tends to be an asset in a garden, since it offers the possibility of introducing an exciting range of plants.
The minimum depth for a small garden pond (up to about 6 m/20 ft in diameter) will need to be about 80 cm (32 in); in the case of larger ponds, depths of up to 1.5 m (5 ft) may be attained. The size and depth of the pond will determine the choice of plants.

Lotus flower (Nelumbo lutea)
This exotic beauty is very sensitive and requires a sunny position, sheltered from the wind. It should be kept in a greenhouse during the winter.

There is little sense in packing a small pond with large plants or, conversely, stocking a large pond with species that remain small.

The floor of the pond and water quality

The floor of the pond will affect the environment of the pond plants quite considerably, no matter whether the chosen material covers the entire bottom of the pond or is used only as compost in plant containers. When deciding on substances, both the nutrient content and the particle size of the material are important factors.

Nutrient content: Use material with few nutrients for the floor of the pond, the best being a sand-loam-gravel mixture (from a gravel pit – not garden soil). Special pond material can be obtained in the gardening trade. Do try to make sure that it does not contain any peat as the exploitation of natural peat bogs destroys the natural habitats of many rare plants. If you

introduce many nutrients to a pond through using rich soil, etc. you will only succeed in discolouring the water with algae (see Fertilizing, p. 20). Nutrients from this soil will dissolve in water and be taken over by algae before the water plants get a chance to use them.

Degree of acidity: The type of substance used for the floor will also influence the degree of acidity (the pH factor) of your garden pond (see p. 20) and, with it, your choice of plants. Any specific pH requirements of individual plants are listed in the plant descriptions on pages 34–59.

Fish in your pond: If you decide to keep fish in your pond, you will need a few technical appliances, such as a filter. In a pond without any technical gadgets or devices, keep the number of fish to a minimum. If you really wish to have a fish pond rather than a garden pond then you should consult specialist literature on the subject. Without any technical aids, the well-

being of both fish and water plants might be affected.

Areas of life in a pond

Four separate natural areas of life (biotopes) can be distinguished in a garden pond, all of which must be taken into consideration when designing and planning the pond (see illustration below). Each biotope offers rather specific conditions to plants, therefore many particular plants are available for each different area (see pp. 34–59).

The marginal zone

A large number of plants and fauna can be established in the marginal (marshy) zone, provided the pond is large enough and is situated in the sunniest part of the garden. Measuring from the surface of the water to the pond liner, the marginal zone should be flat, have a depth of 0–25 cm (0–10 in) and be covered with approximately 10 cm (4 in) of material (e.g. sand-loam-gravel mixture).

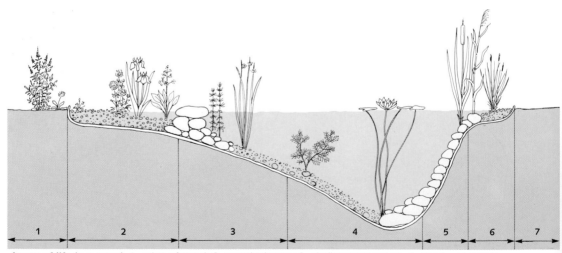

Areas of life in a pond 1. edge of pond; 2. marginal zone; 3. shallow water zone; 4. deep water zone; 5. steep bank; 6. marginal zone; 7. edge of pond.

The shallow water zone

The transitional area between the marginal zone and deep water should not be too steep as otherwise the floor material may slide downwards. Slopes of up to 30 degrees can be covered with fine material; coarser material (e.g. stones with a diameter of up to 15 cm/6 in) is recommended for steeper areas.

The deep water zone

A deep water zone in a pond (of a depth of at least 80 cm/32 in) is essential for some plant species and also for any creatures that will overwinter in the pond. An extended, flat marginal zone in a smaller pond will take up a lot of room. Right at the start, it is a good idea to build a small part of the pond with a steep side so that the required depth can be attained.

The edge of the pond

If the pond liner has been laid properly along the edge of the pond (see p. 9), this area will be just as dry as the rest of the garden. This means that you can plant garden plants here as well. The most suitable plants are those that would naturally grow near water but can still cope with some dryness, e.g. hemp agrimony, yellow loosestrife and creeping Jenny. If your lawn extends to the edge of the pond, a wide band of stones or gravel will prevent the grass from growing into the pond.

Access to the pond is vital. This means placing fewer plants in some places – particularly on a sight-line, or making part of the edge of the pond suitable for walking on by installing flat stones or paving slabs. A broad, pond-edge zone stocked with lots of plants should also be designed. Well-spaced stepping stones will also facilitate the care of plants in areas of denser growth.

Use only nutrient-poor soil for the edge of the pond. Heavy rain might easily wash soil into the pond and this could cause the water to acquire too many nutrients. Plants which cannot manage on nutrient-poor soil should have some garden soil added round their roots when planting to start them off.

What are pond plants?

There is a vast range of plants for use in designing garden ponds so it is useful to know something about them in order to choose the right ones and care for them properly. There are two large groups of pond plants:
- water plants;
- marginal plants.

Water plants

These are divided up into:
- submerged, oxygenating plants (underwater plants) that are completely submerged, rooted in the pond floor and are planted in deep or shallow water zones;
- surface plants whose leaves float on the surface of the water. These plants also possess other, underwater leaves of a different shape. They root in the pond floor and belong in the deep or shallow water zones;
- floating plants that float on the surface of the water and usually do not have any roots in the pond floor. Water soldier (see p. 56) is an exception to this rule because it is free-floating but forms roots during the autumn, which it uses to pull itself down to the bottom for overwintering. Floating plants prefer a deep water zone.

Marginal plants

Either the roots of these plants are under the water or the lowest parts of their stalks are under water. The marshy marginal zone is their natural habitat.

Algae

Algae are also pond plants and, if left to their own devices, will colonize any pond by themselves. As long as they do not get out of hand, they perform a valuable service in garden ponds as natural oxygen and food providers for pond creatures.

Filamentous algae: Very often filamentous algae will proliferate wildly in a newly installed garden pond and float on the top in the form of algae "cushions". They should be fished out occasionally with a net or by hand to prevent them blocking sunlight from underwater plants.

Floating algae: The excess proliferation of algae floating freely in water is also undesirable. They are not always visible to the naked eye but tend to make the water cloudy and may cause a biological inversion in the water (see p. 20).

Other algae: Provided they are kept in check, they will do no harm in your garden pond.

The purpose of plants in a garden pond

Pond plants are not only an attractive accessory but also form a habitat for pond creatures. One of their most important functions is to keep the water clear and prevent algae from taking over. They do this by absorbing nutrients dissolved in the water, thereby withdrawing a means of nourishment from undesirable algae. Underwater plants are particularly effective in this respect. Their large leaf-surface area also ensures that floating particles are caught, thereby helping to keep the water clean. Underwater plants also contribute towards enriching the amount of oxygen in the pond by releasing it into the water where pond creatures and micro-organisms can benefit from it.

Planting aids

It is a good idea to plan ahead for a plant-friendly design when building your pond. This will mean creating as many different planting opportunities as possible for pond plants. Even ready-made ponds that have not been installed in the optimal way can be improved later on.

A pond with a proper floor
(illustration 1)
If you want a proper pond floor in your pond, you can use various different materials, depending on the slope of the floor. Fine material, such as sand and loam, should only be placed in the flat, marginal zone as it will begin to slide even on a very gradual slope. Do not rely on the plants' roots holding on to the material of the pond floor. The finer material will have slid down to the deepest parts of the pond long before the root system has become dense enough. The best material for a shallow marginal zone is a sand-loam-gravel mixture. This nutrient-poor material should be placed in the pond to a thickness of about 10 cm (4 in). The material should be inserted right up to the edge of the pond along the outer edge of the marginal zone so that no water can be seen. A mixture of a little loam and many stones is suitable for the pond floor in the shallow water zone. Place a layer of at least 5 cm (2 in) on top of the pond liner. Very steep banks can be designed with the help of a drystone wall.

Drystone walls for steep banks
(illustration 2)
If the marginal zone borders on a steep bank, there is a risk that the pond floor material will slide down into the pond depths. A drystone wall will support the floor of the marginal zone and camouflage the pond liner all in one. As their rhizomes find a hold on it, plants from the marginal zone and the shallow water zone will colonize the drystone wall. In the case of a ready-made pond, first drain the water.
● Acquire a few natural stones, 10–20 cm (4–8 in) in diameter, from a quarry or gravel works, along with a few larger blocks with a diameter of about 35 cm (14 in).
● Do not trample on and squash the edges of your pond when installing the stones. Nor should you run your wheelbarrow across the pond liner. A helper should be available to hand the stones and other items to you across the liner.

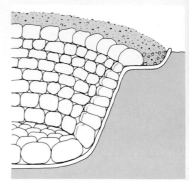

2. Drystone wall, made of stacked-up natural stones.

● Lay the largest stones in the deepest place. Play with the positions of the stones until they are all firmly slotted together.
● Stack further, smaller stones in the gaps (never lay large stones on top of small stones).
● In this fashion, gradually build a wall right up to the top edge of the steep bank.
● Finally, use large stones to support the floor of the neighbouring marginal zone.

Containers as planting aids
Steep banks can be covered with plants quite easily if you use plant containers that can be hooked into the bank or that can be placed on the floor of the pond. Alternatively, you could use verge matting for planting.

Hanging boxes
(illustration 3)
These boxes are suitable for a pond that has been built in an old swimming pool or is flanked by a patio. They are fitted with attachments like those for balcony boxes, and are hooked into the bank in such a way that they are covered by the water. Anchor the fixtures with special dowels on the outside of the pond or on the inside of the wall.

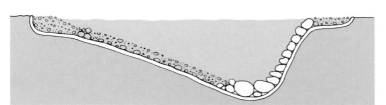

1. Pond floor: use sand-loam-gravel mixture for the marginal zone, loam with stones for the shallow water zone and drystone wall for the steep bank.

Plant containers
(illustration 4)
Plant containers can also be installed as "islands" in the centre of the pond. Use U-shaped building stones as pedestals. (These can be acquired from builders' merchants.) Pad the pond liner with an extra piece of liner (folded to three thicknesses), before standing a U-shaped building stone on the bottom, in order to prevent any damage to the pond liner. The depth at which the container should be immersed in the water will depend on what plants you choose (see Planting in containers, p. 17).
Verge matting (illustration, p. 28): Basically, this consists of loose coconut matting with pockets for inserting plants. It is fixed to the edge of the pond with special dowels, which can usually be purchased together with the verge matting. The pockets of the matting should be filled with a nutrient-poor sand-loam-gravel mixture. Suitable plants can be inserted into this loose weave both above and under the water. Marginal plants that form rhizomes are particularly suitable.

Laying the pond liner along the edge of the pond
In many garden ponds, the pond liner ends up lying flat on the ground at the edge of the pond. However, it is preferable to have the edges of the liner stand up vertically (see illustration 6 and below).

Pond liner that is left flat
(illustration 5)
This simply merges the edge of the pond and the marginal zone. During a drought, the plants along the edge of the pond will absorb a lot of water from the pond and the marginal area may end up drying out completely. There may be considerable fluctuations in water level and few marginal plants can cope with such changes in moisture levels (see pp. 34–59).

Pond liner that stands up vertically
(illustration 6)
If the water level is not allowed to fluctuate too much, you will have the choice of a larger selection of plants for the marginal zone. This also means that there will be no merging of the marginal zone and the edge of the pond. Dig away soil vertically to one spade's depth along the edge of the marginal zone, so that the pond liner stands upright along the edge. The pond liner should end at the same level as the edge of the pond. It can be camouflaged with stones.

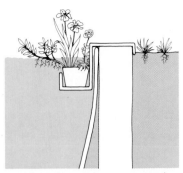

3. A hanging box can be secured with attachments intended for balcony boxes.

4. A plant container can be placed in the pond like a plant island on a U-shaped stone.

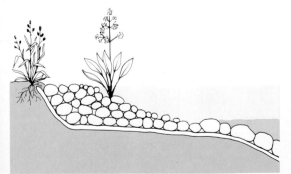

5. A pond liner that finishes lying flat at the edges may create great fluctuations in water levels.

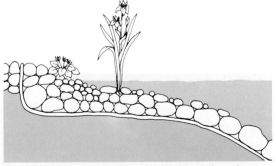

6. A pond liner that stands up vertically at the edges will make sure that the marginal zone stays moist.

Life in and beside water

Pond plants have adapted wonderfully to life in water or to having waterlogged roots.

Water plants have very soft leaves that are not covered with a waxy layer like those of land plants. This enables water plants to absorb nutrients and carbon dioxide directly from the water. The leaves of underwater plants have also developed a large surface area so that they can absorb as many nutrients as possible from the water. This gives them very individual shapes and they are usually more delicate and much more diversified in shape than floating leaves.

Many water plants have a well-developed, air-conducting tissue in their stalks, which acts as a respiration and flotation aid. On the one hand, the air in the tissues gives the leaves buoyancy and enables the plants to remain on the surface of the water. On the other hand, the rhizomes (shoots with a rooting function) and the roots of the plants are supplied with oxygen from the air, which is being absorbed by the leaves and conducted downwards through the stalks. Even in oxygen-poor soil, it is possible for water plants to survive quite happily.

Marginal plants often have large, delicate leaves that provide them with the facility for adequate transpiration in a moist environment. This is necessary for filtering and transporting water containing dissolved nutrients: the nutrients will be filtered out during transportation and the water then evaporates from the surface of the leaves.

Dragonflies mating.

Botanical miracles

Water plants are quite astonishing in their ability to do unusual things. It is interesting to discover that, in fact, these plants do not derive directly from ancient plants that also grew in water. They were all previously land plants that have adapted to life in water. The development of increasingly large numbers of plant species on land caused great competition for survival, which some plants avoided by adapting to life in wet areas. Gradual mutation and change enabled them to diversify and penetrate wetter habitats until they ended up adapting entirely to life in water. This evolution can be seen quite clearly in the example of amphibious bistort (see p. 55). Unlike many other water plants, it has not entirely given up life on land, but is able to grow as a water or land version depending on its position in the environment. This plant is, therefore, referred to as an amphibian.

It was necessary for plants that were used to life on land to make considerable adaptations for their "step back" into water.
● They learned to float.
● They are able to perform an exchange of carbon dioxide and oxygen underwater.
● They are able to absorb nutrients not only through their roots but also through their leaves directly from water.
● Their leaves are not equipped with a water-impermeable wax layer as this would hinder any kind of exchange of gases from the surrounding water.
● Flowering, pollination and the distribution of seed are all possible underwater.

Propagation without flowers

Propagation from seed is a fairly unfavourable method for flowering plants that live underwater. A deficiency in oxygen supply on the floor of the pond will often cause the seeds to die, which is why flowering plants in a pond usually propagate by means of rhizomes and the branching of rhizomes. It also means that lots of water plants of one species always grow together in dense groups, while in the case of land plants that propagate from seed, many very different species can grow in a small space.

Propagation by means of rhizomes also occurs very often among non-flowering water plants. For example, the *Chara* species of algae (see p. 58) form a dense underwater carpet, which often completely obscures the bottoms of cleaner, light-permeable waters.

Rootless survivors

Some water plants, such as common bladderwort and hornwort species, no longer form any kind of roots. These plants are very successful cleaners of the water in garden ponds, as they absorb nutrients dissolved in the water through their leaves alone. In this way, they use up more nutrients from pond water than plants that root in the bottom. Rigid hornwort (see p. 58) is only present in water that contains sufficient dissolved nutrients for its nourishment. Common bladderwort (see p. 59) will also colonize clear water with low quantities of dissolved nutrients as it is able to catch and digest small creatures, such as water-fleas, as a supplement to its diet. This carnivorous plant has adapted some of its leaves into small bladders with a low internal pressure. Fine hairs situated around the surface "trapdoor" entrance of this bladder react to the touch of these minute water creatures by opening suddenly. The influx of water pulls the water-flea into the bladder, the trapdoor closes and the creature is digested.

Nourishment from the air

Nitrogen is a vital element of nutrition among all plants. Most water plants rely on nitrogen compounds dissolved in the water and on the pond floor. Blue algae, however, are able to absorb nitrogen directly from the air. Eventually, through various biological processes of decay and redistribution, this nitrogen will be made available to all the plants in the pond.

Underwater flowers

These can be seen in rigid hornwort, for example. Underwater flowers are actually fairly inconspicuous as they do not need to attract insects for pollination purposes as land flowers do with their splendid, colourful and scented petals and other parts. As a rule, water insects are carnivorous, preying on other insects and water creatures, and would, therefore, not collect pollen from flowers.

Overwintering buds

Some underwater plants form small buds in order to survive the winter. These buds drop off, are buried in the mud at the bottom of the pond and are thus protected from freezing to death. These over-wintering buds come to life again in the spring to produce new plants of common bladderwort, frog bit or water soldier, for example. The overwintering buds are small and inconspicuous so, when clearing out dead matter from the bottom of the pond in autumn, you must take care that these buds are not damaged.

The never-ending fascination of a garden pond

There is room for a garden pond in even the smallest garden. This garden is only 300 m (3,222 sq ft), and the rounded pond fits in harmoniously. A luxuriant planting of garden flowers along the edges, interesting grasses and the paved sitting area make this pond a favourite haunt for the whole family.

Iris ensata 'Embosed' is a variety of Japanese iris. It grows to a height of 1 m (40 in) and requires humus-rich, acid soil.

How to create the perfect garden pond

An enormous range of attractive, colourful plants for garden ponds is offered for sale. It is up to you to choose the right plants and to plant them in the right place so that your garden pond is green and full of flowers from the spring until the autumn.

The 12 golden rules for planting in and around a garden pond

1. When buying plants, check the flowering times of individual species and varieties (see pp. 34–59) if you want to ensure plenty of flowers around your garden pond from spring to autumn.
2. When you buy water-lilies do not be surprised by their unpleasant smell. Very often, the end of the rootstock has died off and is decaying. This is a perfectly normal process in water-lilies and will not detract from their well-being.
3. Do not be deceived by the small size of water plants when buying them. They will soon grow into splendid plants.
4. Plant no more than ten specimens of smaller species, and no more than five plants per square metre (see pp. 34–59 for details of individual plants).
5. Do not install very tall species of plants such as reeds or broad-leafed reedmace in small garden ponds.
6. Use small plants for the part of the pond that is in your immediate line of sight (e.g. from a patio).

7. Do not mix plants of different sizes and heights within a group. The small plants will quickly become completely overshadowed by the larger ones and will be crowded out.
8. Plant small species in groups so that they are not crowded out by larger species.
9. Do not plant very tall plants on the sunny side of the pond, since they will then overshadow the smaller ones.
10. Underwater plants belong in every garden pond as they will improve the quality of the water.
11. Do not add extra nutrients to the pond in the form of fertilizer and nutrient-rich soil, as this will only encourage the growth of algae.
12. If you want frogs, toads and newts to colonize your pond, plant one side of the pond with a dense grouping of shrubs to create an undisturbed habitat for them.
NB: If you also own a running stream and are looking for suitable plants, you will find tips among the plant descriptions (see pp. 34–59).

When to plant in and around your pond
You can install plants in your garden pond from spring to autumn. The last month of spring and the first month of summer are ideal times for new planting or additional planting as the plants will then be able to acclimatize to their new surroundings at the beginning of their growth season and will show themselves off in full splendour during the course of the summer. However, even plants planted in the middle of summer will still grow well, although you will probably not be able to enjoy their beautiful flowers until the following summer.
NB: If you plant in early spring or late autumn, you run the risk of setting plants too close together. Plants that form overwintering buds (see p. 11), will be unable to do so if first planted in late autumn.

Where to buy pond plants
Garden centres, aquarium suppliers and specialist water plant garden centres usually have a large range of pond plants for sale. You can also order pond plants via plant mail order firms.
NB: Please do not take water plants from the wild as you would almost certainly damage their natural habitat and possibly also break the law in the case of protected species. The vast range of plants offered by the gardening trade makes this latter route quite unnecessary.

What to watch for when buying water plants
Before deciding on a particular plant, make sure that you find out about its requirements as to care. The amount of time spent on care can vary greatly, particularly for the overwintering of water-lilies (see p. 24). Check the plants carefully and watch for the following:

A successful combination of delicate blue and fresh yellow flowers in a deep green setting.

● all pond plants should have young shoots or buds. They should not have too many bent stalks or leaves. If there are just a few, simply cut them off when you are planting them;

● water plants are allowed to look brown and unattractive to begin with, but should not be decaying (except for water-lilies). They will quickly recover in the right position;

● the rootstocks of marginal plants should be vigorous. If the young shoots have progressed too far, they should be cut back.

Transportation of plants

Pond plants should be planted as soon as possible as storing them for a long time may damage them. *Surface plants* can be transported in a bucket of water. Use a large container on a long journey so that the floating leaves can lie on the surface of the water. A plastic bag will suffice for short distances. *Floating plants* can be transported in a bucket of water. For short journeys, use a plastic bag. *Submerged, oxygenating plants* (underwater plants) should be

transported in a large container and covered with water. Store them for a brief period only. If they are kept densely packed for too long, they will die because of lack of light. *Marginal plants* should be transported with their roots immersed in water or at least protected from drying out with a plastic bag. If they are stored for a long time, their roots should be in water. They should not stand too close together.

Planting suggestions

The illustration below shows a model pond with a diameter of about 6 m (20 ft) at its widest point. It is divided up into areas marked A to J, each of which is supplied with suggestions for the number and species of plants.

A Marginal zone (sunny, low-growing plants, on sight line): 5 water mint (*Mentha aquatica*), 3 brooklime (*Veronica beccabunga*), 1 water forget-me-not (*Myosotis scorpioides*), 2 marsh marigold (*Caltha palustris*), 2 blue iris (*Iris sibirica*), 3 bog bean (*Menyanthes trifoliata*), 3 tufted loosestrife (*Lysimachia thyrsiflora*), 3 creeping Jenny (*Lysimachia nummularia*), 2 mare's tail (*Hippuris vulgaris*).

B Marginal zone (semi-shady, slightly taller plants): 2 common bistort (*Polygonum bistorta*), 3 broad-leaved cotton grass (*Eriophorum latifolium*), 3 common flag (*Iris pseudacorus*), 5 spike rush (*Eleocharis palustris*), 1 globeflower (*Trollius europaeus*).

C Marginal zone (sunny, tall plants): 1 common flag (*Iris pseudacorus*), 3 skullcap (*Scutellaria galericulata*), 2 arrow-head (*Sagittaria sagittifolia*), 1 amphibious bistort (*Polygonum amphibium*), 1 bog arum (*Calla palustris*), 2 branched bur-weed (*Sparganium erectum*), 2 pendulous sedge (*Carex pendula*).

D Marginal zone (sunny to semi-shady, tall plants): 2 purple moor-grass (*Molinia caerulea*), 2 butterbur (*Petasites hybridus*).

E Marginal zone (semi-shady, tall plants to provide a margin): 2 hemp agrimony (*Eupatorium cannabinum*), 1 common reed (*Phragmites australis*), 2 meadow-sweet (*Filipendula ulmaria*).

F Shallow water zone: 2 greater spearwort (*Ranunculus lingua*), 3 water fringe (*Nymphoides peltata*), 2 water crowfoot (*Ranunculus aquatilis*), 1 broad-leaved pondweed (*Potamogeton natans*), 2 water violet (*Hottonia palustris*), 3 algae (*Chara* spp.), 2 marsh cinquefoil (*Potentilla palustris*).

G Deep water zone: 1 water-lily (*Nymphaea alba*), 1 yellow water-lily (*Nuphar lutea*), 3 water milfoil (*Myriophyllum verticillatum*), 3 rigid hornwort (*Ceratophyllum demersum*), 3 Canadian pondweed (*Elodea canadensis*), 3 common bladderwort (*Utricularia vulgaris*).

H Plant island (diameter of container about 1 m (40 in):

2 common reed (*Phragmites australis*), 3 bulrush (*Scirpus lacustris*), 2 flowering rush (*Butomus umbellatus*), 5 mare's tail (*Hippuris vulgaris*), 2 reedmace (*Typha latifolia*); beside container 3 water soldier (*Stratiotes aloides*).

I Edge of pond (southern edge, sight line): 1 yellow loosestrife (*Lysimachia punctata*), 1 tansy (*Tanacetum vulgare*), 3 Japanese iris (*Iris ensata*), 5 water mint (*Mentha aquatica*), 3 creeping Jenny (*Lysimachia nummularia*).

K Edge of pond (north-facing side): 1 hemp agrimony (*Eupatorium cannabinum*), 1 meadowsweet (*Filipendula ulmaria*), 3 great willowherb (*Epilobium hirsutum*), 1 *Aruncus dioicus*.

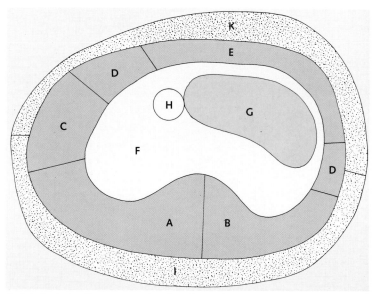

A detailed planting suggestion for all pond zones A–E = marginal zone; F = shallow water zone; G = deep water zone; H = planting island; I and K = edge of pond.

Planting in containers

Plant containers make it possible to create islands in a pond. They can also be used in a pond without a proper floor. Hanging boxes are also very practical (see p. 9).

A container of reed plants: diameter about 1 m (40 in), in 20 cm (8 in) of water.
● 6 common reed (*Phragmites australis*), 10 bulrush (*Scirpus lacustris*), 6 mare's tail (*Hippuris vulgaris*) or;
● 5 reedmace (*Typha latifolia*), 10 bulrush (*Scirpus lacustris*), 3 reed sweet-grass (*Glyceria maxima*), 3 water soldier (*Stratiotes aloides*).

Flower container: diameter about 80 cm (32 in), in 10 cm (4 in) of water.
● 3 lesser reedmace (*Typha angustifolia*), 4 common flag (*Iris pseudacorus*), 6 mare's tail (*Hippuris vulgaris*), 3 bogbean (*Menyanthes trifoliata*) or;
● 3 purple loosestrife (*Lythrum salicaria*), 2 water plantain (*Alisma plantago-aquatica*), 3 marsh cinquefoil (*Potentilla palustris*), 5 mare's tail (*Hippuris vulgaris*).

Hanging boxes: about 1 m (40 in) long.
● Low-growing, cushion-forming planting: 2 marsh marigold (*Caltha palustris*), 3 marsh forget-me-not (*Myosotis scorpioides*), 3 brooklime (*Veronica beccabunga*), 5 creeping Jenny (*Lysimachia nummularia*), 3 bogbean (*Menyanthes trifoliata*).
● Medium high planting: 3 cotton grass (*Eriophorum latifolium*), 2 globeflower (*Trollius europaeus*), 5 blue iris (*Iris sibirica*), 3 marsh cinquefoil (*Potentilla palustris*), 3 bogbean (*Menyanthes trifoliata*).
● Tall planting: 3 common flag (*Iris pseudacorus*), 1 tufted sedge (*Carex elata*), 2 water plantain (*Alisma plantago-aquatica*), with 5 marsh forget-me-not (*Myosotis scorpioides*).

Plants for a shaded pond

Only special, shade-loving plant species will be able to flourish in a garden pond that is partially shaded by deciduous trees. Never install a garden pond in the deep shade of dense conifers.

Plant name	Depth of water	Number per m²
watercress (*Nasturtium officinale*)	0–3 cm (0–1¼ in)	5
floating sweet-grass (*Glyceria fluitans*)	0–5 cm (0–2 in)	2
common flag (*Iris pseudacorus*)	0–10 cm (0–4 in)	3
common reed (*Phragmites australis*)	0–30 cm (0–12 in)	5
shining pondweed (*Potamogeton lucens*)	30–80 cm (12–32 in)	2*
pendulous sedge (*Carex pendula*)	0–10 cm (0–4 in)	2
curled pondweed (*Potamogeton crispus*)	20–50 cm (8–20 in)	4*
butterbur (*Petasites hybridus*)	0 cm	2
arrowhead (*Sagittaria sagittifolia*)	0–20 cm (0–8 in)	2
creeping Jenny (*Lysimachia nummularia*)	0–10 cm (0–4 in)	5
rigid hornwort (*Ceratophyllum demersum*)	floating	5
cyperus sedge (*Carex pseudocyperus*)	0–10 cm (0–4 in)	2
flowering rush (*Butomus umbellatus*)	0–10 cm (0–4 in)	5
broad-leaved pondweed (*Potamogeton natans*)	from 40 cm (16 in)	3*
marsh cinquefoil (*Potentilla palustris*)	10–40 cm (4–16 in)	2
bog arum (*Calla palustris*)	0 cm	2
marsh marigold (*Caltha palustris*)	0–5 cm (0–2 in)	2
marsh fern (*Thelypteris palustris*)	0–3 cm (0–1¼ in)	2
mare's tail (*Hippuris vulgaris*)	5–20 cm (2–8 in)	5*
reed sweet-grass (*Glyceria maxima*)	0–20 cm (0–8 in)	2

* plant in groups

Planting

Planting in the pond floor
Consider the plants' requirements as to position and nutrients (see pp. 34–59).

Undemanding pond plants
(illustration 1)
Plants with low nutrient requirements can be planted straight into the floor of the pond without any additional compost.
● Cut off any bent stalks below the bend.
● Always cut back the roots a little, even if they are short. This gets rid of incipient decay, prevents the roots from bending in the planting hole, and encourages root growth.
● Use a small spade to make a planting hole in the floor of the pond. It should be only a little larger than the rootstock.
● Insert the plant, fill the hole with material already dug from the floor and make sure that the neck of the rootstock is just about covered with material.

Demanding pond plants
(illustration 2)
In a newly built garden pond, the supply of nutrients will probably be inadequate for some plants. This means that the plants will need a starter boost of nutrient-rich, fertilizer-free garden soil placed in their planting hole.
● Cut off bent stalks below the bend.
● Shorten the roots.
● Dig the planting hole about 5 cm (2 in) deeper and wider than the rootstock.
● Hold the rootstock in the hole with one hand and use the other hand to shovel in as much garden soil as is needed to cover the top of the rootstock. Press down the soil.
● Cover the soil with a layer of gravel to help to keep the nutrients around the roots and prevent them from escaping into the surrounding water. The layer of gravel should not be higher than the lowest leaves of the plants.

The pH factor
A few pond plants have special requirements with respect to the acid/alkaline ratio of the water they live in. The higher the pH factor, the higher the alkaline (lime) content. Plants that need lime, such the blue iris (see p. 44), should receive a little lime together with nutrient-rich soil in their planting hole. A plant such as bog arum (*Calla palustris*) (see p. 38), which does not like lime, should be given a little well-rotted bark mulch instead of nutrient-rich soil. We recommend repeating this procedure every one to two years if the plants do not seem to thrive.

Plants in containers
Plant containers are well suited for creating small islands in a pond, even in ponds without a proper floor. They can also be used for planting non-hardy plants which can then be removed from the pond quite easily in the autumn. Planting suggestions will be found on page 17.

Open and closed plant containers
The plant containers offered for sale in the gardening trade are mainly basket-mesh containers. They are recommended for plants that have to be removed from a pond for overwintering, as they are not too heavy and the water is able to run away quite easily. The drawback is that nutrients can also escape easily into the water. To avoid this problem, it is a good idea to line the baskets with a fabric liner, which can be purchased in the gardening trade.

Closed containers make it harder for air to reach the roots but in any case most pond plants possess special air-conducting tissues (see p. 10) as oxygen is usually in short supply around their roots in their natural habitat.

The right size of container: The container should have a diameter of 80–120 cm (32–60 in) for use as a plant island, while a diameter of 40 cm (16 in) will be sufficient for individual plants.

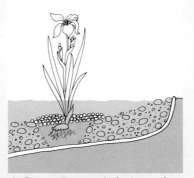

1. Undemanding pond plants can be planted without adding compost.

2. Demanding pond plants need nutrient-rich soil or compost.

3. Line all baskets with a suitable interfacing fabric.

How to plant in containers
(illustrations 3 and 4)
● Line the basket with fabric liner so that no soil can escape into the water.
● Fill the basket with nutrient-poor compost (sand-loam-gravel mixture) and add garden soil to the root-stocks of demanding plants.
● Cut off any overhanging fabric and fold the edge to the inside.
● Cover the surface of the compost with a layer of gravel.

Planting pond plants with rhizomes
The rhizomes of pond plants need to lie horizontally, whether the plants are placed in a container or planted in the floor of the pond. The rhizome contains air and will have to be weighted down with stones so that it does not rise to the surface. Cut back all roots before planting.

4. Cover the compost with a layer of gravel.

5. Plant the rhizomes of water-lilies horizontally.

Planting water-lilies
(illustration 5)
Non-hardy water-lilies are best planted in containers as they can then be taken out of the pond for overwintering. Hardy species can be planted in the pond floor. Make sure the rhizomes are laid in a horizontal position. Always add a little nutrient-rich soil when planting water-lilies, but no fertilizer. Detailed instructions for the care of water-lilies can be found on page 23.

Later planting
(illustration 6)
If you want to add water plants to your pond later on, there is a useful trick to make this easy. Tie the plant securely to a stone with a bit of string and allow this "planting stone" to sink to the bottom in the chosen position. Water-lilies can also be added in this way later on. Sink the plant carefully with the help of a garden fork so that you can make sure that the rhizome ends up horizontal on the pond floor. In a mature pond, there is no need to add an extra supply of nutrients.

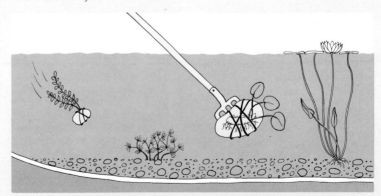

6. Tie submerged oxygenating plants and water-lilies to a stone with string and sink them in the pond.

Creating a green and flowering pond

Care of the plants should not take up much time if you have stocked your garden pond with plants in the correct way. You will then be able to enjoy your pond to the utmost during the summer months, as care will be restricted to a few measures. Propagating pond plants is very straighforward once you know how to go about it.

Pond plants can be planted with the help of plant containers (e.g. mesh baskets), in hanging boxes or in verge matting along the edge of the pond. There is hardly any difference in care.

Fertilizing

You should not add any extra nutrients to the pond, so you must avoid any kind of fertilizer in order not to encourage the growth of floating algae. The nutrients already contained in the water and in the pond floor will be quite sufficient for nourishing your pond plants.

Too many nutrients can be harmful

Unlike in flowerbeds, too many nutrients in a garden pond are positively undesirable. Poor-quality water and a cloudy brew would be the inevitable result. Marginal plants would continue to flourish but underwater plants and pond creatures might find such a change in the water lethal. In extreme cases, the "death" of

the pond may result. To begin with, excess nutrients would encourage excessive growth of algae. The water would turn green and cloudy and light would only be able to penetrate the upper regions. The lack of light would soon cause the algae and under-water plants to die. Their decomposition by bacteria and fungi would lead to a complete depletion of oxygen. The bacteria responsible for decay would multiply and the pond would begin to stink of rotten eggs.

Do not fertilize along the edge of the pond

Avoid using fertilizers that dissolve easily, even along the dry part of the edge of the pond. If put here they would be washed into the pond every time it rains. Species along the edge of the pond, which require plenty of nutrients, can be given a little compost that will release nutrients very slowly. Use it sparingly, however, so that it does not turn into a constant source of nutrients for the pond.

The acidity of the pond water

You should not ignore the degree of acidity (the pH factor) of the pond water during pond care. A certain amount of acid and alkaline substances are always dissolved in any natural body of water. If the water contains more acid than alkaline substances it will be acid and have a pH value below 7. Water in which acids and alkalines are in balance is chemically neutral and corresponds to a pH value of 7.

During the course of natural development, the pH value of a pond will generally decrease, which means that it will become slightly acid (pH 6–6.9). The reason for this is that acid rain and increased plant growth affect the pH factor. This slight change is usually of no consequence to pond plants.

Plants with special demands

A few plants prefer a pH value above 8, which means that you should add a little lime to the rootstock. The lime will neutralize the acid. Plants that only flourish in very acid soil (pH value below 5) can be given a little well-rotted bark mulch around their rootstocks.

View from a patio

In the background is a luxuriant, tall-growing grouping of plants; in the foreground, a small "forest" of mare's tail and a footpath along the edge made of gravel and natural boulders.

Care

Thinning out and cutting back

It is essential to thin out and cut back fast-growing pond plants as the plants tend to reduce the surface area of free water and rob other plants of space and light. Dead and decaying plant stalks should also be removed as they interfere with the quality of the water.

Cutting rhizomes of plants in island containers

(illustration 1)
Rhizomes that are growing out into the pond are extremely visible and easy to cut off. It is best to use a tree-pruning tool with a long handle, with which you will be able to reach plants quite easily from the edge of the pond. Such a tool can be obtained from any good gardening shop or centre. Cut off all rhizomes that are growing further than 30 cm (12 in) outside of the container. Cut those that are hanging over the edge of the container only so much that they still cover the edge.

Cutting reeds

(illustration 2)
Use a sharp knife to cut the thick stalks of reeds. Hedge clippers are also suitable for cutting reedmace. Cut off the plant stalks about 5 cm (2 in) above the surface of the water, otherwise the plant will decay.

Cutting back fast-growing marginal plants in the pond floor

(illustration 3)
If marginal plants start to grow too far towards the middle of the pond, the rhizomes should be cut off as near to the edge of the marginal zone as possible. If you cannot reach rhizomes growing into the pond floor, cut off the young plants that have grown too far into the middle, making sure you cut them as near to the rhizomes as possible and under the surface of the water.

Underwater plants as nutrient traps

Use plenty of underwater plants in your garden pond. They grow fast and will absorb lots of nutrients. If they grow too much, however, you should remove about half of the total quantity in late summer. This

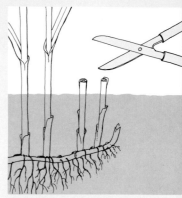

2. Reed stems can be cut off about 5 cm (2 in) above the surface of the water.

will reduce the nutrient supply of the pond. Use a rake with blunt teeth for this operation. The underwater plants that have been removed should be stacked in a heap very close to the pond for about a day, in order to enable any water creatures that have been scooped up by mistake to find their way back into the pond.

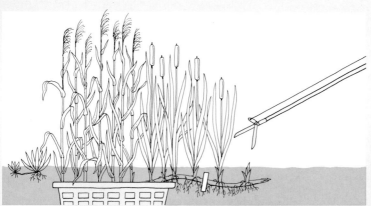

1. Rhizomes that proliferate too far into the pond should be cut off. Use tree cutters for plants on a planting island.

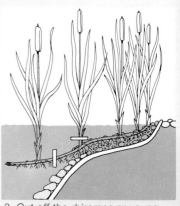

3. Cut off the rhizomes or young plantlets of marginal plants.

Care of water-lilies

Water-lilies have different requirements for care depending on the species. The white water-lily (*Nymphaea alba*) is very robust and easy to care for, while tropical species and some cultivars are very sensitive and will only flourish under optimum conditions (see p. 54).

Care of rhizomes
(illustrations 4 and 5)
Before planting the rhizome, remove all decaying parts. The end of the rhizome will nearly always be decayed, which is easily recognizable by the bad smell and the soft, spongy tissue. Use a sharp knife to shorten the rhizome so that all decayed roots are removed. Decayed parts in the front part of the rhizomes should also be completely cut out. A budding knife is useful for cutting out small patches. Protect the wounds from further decay by using a paintbrush to apply active charcoal or charcoal powder on to the cut surfaces.

Stacked leaves
(illustration 6)
If plants have become too dense, are creating too much shade or the water is becoming too shallow, the water-lilies will begin to stack their leaves on top of each other and produce very few flowers. If there is too much shade or the water is too shallow, you should take the plants out and plant them in a more favourable position. If the plants have become too dense, either take out individual plants or cut leaves off some of the stronger ones. Do not tear off the water-lily leaves as this might damage the rhizome. Instead, cut off the leaf stalks with sharp scissors or tree clippers, under the water and close above the rhizome.

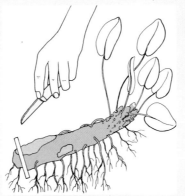

4. Remove all decaying parts before planting.

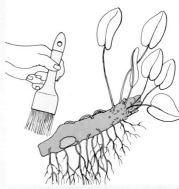

5. Paint active charcoal or charcoal powder on all cut surfaces.

Dividing rhizomes
Even if the water-lilies are in a good position and have enough room, the leaves may end up growing above each other and riding up. If this occurs, a rejuvenation cut will help. This operation should be carried out in the autumn or spring. Remove the entire plant from the pond and cut off the daughter plants wherever the rhizomes branch out (illustration 2, p. 30). You can prepare the rhizome of the strongest plant for planting, as shown in illustrations 4

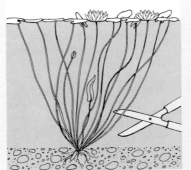

6. Cut off the leaf stalks of water-lilies above the rhizomes.

and 5 (above). Often several water-lily plants will have been created as the connections at branching points have decayed. In this case, take out the weaker ones and only put the strongest ones back into the pond.

Changing the compost
If your water-lilies remain small or do not grow much in spite of a favourable position and plenty of room, they are probably suffering from nutrient deficiency. In such a case, you should change the planting compost. This deficiency does not often occur in plants that grow out of the floor of the pond as, generally, there are enough nutrients at their disposal. Plants in containers, on the other hand, frequently suffer from nutrient deficiency. Remove the plant container from the pond in the autumn or spring and carefully take the plant out. Fill the container with fresh compost (see p. 19).

Thinning out and cutting back the plants

Thinning out and cutting back is not only important in the care of pond plants but also decreases the nutrient content of the pond water. Many nutrients are bound in plant matter and would naturally dissolve back into the water when dead parts of plants decompose. Thinning out or cutting back should be carried out when:
● fast-growing species smother smaller, light-loving plants;
● if you have species in your pond, such as reedmace, which form rhizomes. Cut off the rhizomes growing towards the middle of the pond, otherwise they will rapidly reduce the expanse of open water in smaller ponds;
● if floating plants are growing so vigorously that they are covering large parts of the surface of the water. Fish the plants out or the underwater plants will suffer from light deficiency.

What to watch for when cutting back

● When thinning out marginal plants, make sure to cut them above the surface of the water in order to prevent decay. If you cut them off under the surface of the water, water will penetrate the air-filled tissues and the oxygen supply to rhizomes and roots will suffer. The plant will begin to decay.
● Cut back in a way that will decrease overshadowing of smaller species, which are usually those most in need of plenty of light.
● Plants that do not grow very well should not be cut back much as they might then be overtaken by faster-growing competitors.

Care in the autumn

During the autumn months, the wind will blow dead leaves, cones and various berries, etc. into your garden pond. This will add nutrients to the pond water, which will rapidly cause the quality of the water to deteriorate, particularly in smaller ponds. Dead leaves and parts of plants should be fished out of the pond with a net.

Removing berries, seeds, cones and fallen leaves

Berries and seeds are likely to make the quality of the water deteriorate through decay and fermentation processes, as are cones from conifers, which release resins and tannins that harm pond life. Large numbers of leaves in the pond should always be removed in the autumn by skimming them from the surface of the water. In smaller quantities, leaves are not harmful; they usually decay and decompose and will later serve as a natural source of nutrients for water plants. If berries, cones and foliage have already sunk to the bottom of the pond, use a fishing net to clean the pond floor rather than a rake, which might easily damage water plants or the pond liner.

Overwintering quarters for small creatures

Most pond plants die down in the autumn. If you have planted reeds all around your pond, many dead stalks will protrude from the water. Resist the temptation to cut back all of these hollow stalks as many tiny creatures overwinter inside them. The stalks also serve as an oxygen supplier to the rhizomes when the pond is covered with a thick layer of ice in the winter. If you still want to cut away the dead stalks, wait until spring. After a few warmer days, about the middle of the first month of spring, the little creatures will begin to leave the stalks. Even then, you should only cut the portions of stalks protruding above the surface of the water, so as not to

endanger the oxygen supply to the rhizomes. Watch out for the many marginal plants while cutting back reeds as the young shoots of these plants are fairly inconspicuous and can easily be destroyed.

Overwintering pond plants

How well your pond plants manage to cope with the winter will depend on whether they are hardy or not.

Hardy pond plants

These plants should be over-wintered in the pond. Their roots will then not be damaged, which might otherwise be inevitable if larger plants are removed from the pond. Many pond plants retract in the autumn, which means that they withdraw nutrients from their leaves and transport them to the over-wintering parts such as roots and rhizomes. The leaves will die off. Some species only overwinter in the shape of overwintering buds (see p. 11) and are almost invisible in that state. In all of these cases, you need not worry about the plants as they can look after themselves.

Non-hardy pond plants

Non-hardy plants, such as some water-lily species (see p. 54), are best planted in containers (see p. 19) in your garden pond. This will avoid damaging the roots and other pond plants when they are removed for overwintering in the autumn. Plants growing in containers should be overwintered in a cool but frost-free position, e.g. in a cellar window or a conservatory. The container should be placed underwater in a larger container. In the case of less-sensitive species, you may also cover the plant with dead leaves and leave it standing outside. You only need to water the container during long periods of drought in order to keep the plants constantly moist.

Tropical water-lilies must be over-wintered in a heated water bath at a minimum temperature of 20°C (68°F) and should not be put back into the pond before the end of the last month of spring.

Later planting

A certain basic stock of plants (see Planting suggestions, p. 16) will give the pond its particular character throughout the years. The continuing development of the pond will create the most diverse growing conditions during the first few years. When adding plants later, it is worth reintroducing plants that were unsuccessful in the first few years, since it is quite possible that they may adapt quickly to your now more mature pond. If you want to introduce new plant species to an already well-established pond, it will be sufficient if you merely thin out some of the neighbouring plants to give the newcomers enough light and a chance to establish themselves.

If you have a large stock of fish, you should plant new underwater plants fairly often. Some species of fish prefer soft underwater plants as a food supply.

A unique display of blue irises.

Changing the pond water

A biological balance will be achieved in a well-functioning garden pond and this could be seriously disturbed by such operations as changing the water. There are some situations, however, that make it necessary to change the water:

● if the surface of the water is covered with an oily film and many pond creatures are dying, perhaps because rain water from your house roof has been conducted into the pond. Acidification of the water and a build-up of chemicals may result;

● if a concrete pond was not soaked in water for long enough before plants were introduced and toxic substances have leached from the concrete and are leading to the death of pond creatures.

NB: In all cases, proceed very carefully and only pump out about half of the water, then add fresh water. If the water level has dropped considerably – particularly in the case of small ponds – during long periods of drought, allow fresh water to flow in extremely slowly.

Water filters and aerators

In the case of garden ponds that have been professionally built, and in which there are no or only very few fish, there is no need for filters and water aerators. If they are present because you have a large number of fish in your pond, make sure that the movement of water created by the filter device and aerator is not too strong. Lots of waves created by splashing water will often disturb water plants whose natural habitat consists of still water. Surface plants, such as water-lilies or broad-leaved pondweed (*Potamogeton natans*), will not feel comfortable in such conditions. Make sure that you never use chemical additives in filters!

Switching on the filter again: If a filter is switched on again after a lengthy period of rest, it is necessary to conduct the first surge of water out of the pond. This is because the unused filter will harbour large quantities of organic substances that have been decomposed by bacteria and fungi. These decayed products would otherwise be pumped straight into the pond when the filter is turned on again, causing a lowering of the quality of the water.

Removing a filter: If you decide to remove the filter completely, the transition period will take some time and the pond water will not be very clear during that period. The use of underwater plants which are able to absorb nutrients dissolved in the water through their leaves will accelerate clearing of the water.

Plant protection

Plant protection in and around a garden pond is usually a matter of taking preventive measures. The most important point is the choice of the right position for individual species of plants (see pp. 34–59). Chemical plant protection agents should never be used in the pond as they will considerably and negatively affect the quality of the water and may be toxic to pond creatures. Do not use any biological plant brews or soap solutions either as these may cause great damage to the pond and radically disturb the community of plants and animals. Biological substances, such as herbal brews or soft soap, can be employed along a dry pond edge in exceptional cases. Do not spray these agents in the direction of the water, however, to ensure that none of them ends up in the pond. Completely avoid using any chemical agents on the pond edge. Even after they have been broken down in the soil, they are still present in a different form and may endanger life in the soil or pond.

Diseases and pests

If they are planted in the correct positions, pond plants are rarely infested with diseases and pests.

Mildew

Powdery mildew can occasionally be observed. It tends to infest shrubs around the edge of the pond, for example meadowsweet (see p. 42). Plants that are growing in a position that is too dry are more likely to be affected. The proximity of other plants susceptible to mildew, such as roses, may provoke infestation. Only complete removal of the infested plants will serve in a case of serious attack, so that other plants do not become infested too.

Iris rust

Iris rust (*Puccinia iridae*) is a fungus that attacks certain iris species. This fungus forms yellow-orange spots on the leaves. The species most likely to be infested are those that prefer a moist position and are being grown in a dry one. The best procedure is to destroy the infested plants and to plant new ones in a more favourable position.

Caterpillars

Various water butterflies may prove unwelcome guests around a pond as hungry caterpillars can cause considerable damage to water-lilies. They bite shield-shaped pieces out of the edges of water-lily leaves and build a cocoon in which the larvae pupate until metamorphosing into their adult form (illustration, p. 28). The marks of their voracious feeding are clearly visible on the water-lily leaves. Healthy water-lilies can cope with these parasites. If they should get out of hand, however, simply collect the caterpillars or cocoons by hand or remove the

Iris ensata – the colours and shapes of the petals are quite exquisite.

eaten leaves. Do not use any pest control agents as they are very toxic and would damage the pond.

Galerucella nymphaeae

Another pest that attacks water-lilies is *Galerucella nymphaeae*. This beetle is dark brown and about 1–2 cm ($^1/_2$–$^3/_4$ in) long. It lives along the edge of the pond and eats various pond plants but lays its eggs only on water-lily leaves. The larvae create tunnels in the leaves but there is rarely much damage and the beetle generally appears only in large colonies of water-lilies. In a garden pond, it is a simple matter to collect up the beetles and larvae by hand.

Slugs and snails

Garden slugs and snails are ancient enemies that will sometimes penetrate the marginal zone of a pond. They will keep away if the marginal zone is kept consistently moist and will rarely inflict much damage along the edge of the pond. If they get out of control, simply collect them by hand. Never use toxic slug pellets or any similar product, since it might end up in the pond. If frogs, toads or newts decide to make a home in or around your pond, you will find that they are a great help in keeping down insects and other undesirable pests – but not, of course, if you fill the water with poisons!

What to do when things go wrong

Caterpillar of Nymphula nymphaeata.

Verge matting.

Symptoms	Causes
The water level is particularly low.	Roots from the edge of the pond have penetrated into the pond and are absorbing the water.
	The marginal zone and the edge of the pond have not been properly separated.
	A hole in the pond liner (a stone may have penetrated the liner or, more rarely, the liner has been torn open by a sheet of ice).
Marginal plants begin to die.	Diseases, infestation with pests, damage by snails.
	The marginal zone is drying out at times.
Water-lily leaves will not float, but tend to pile up.	Plants are not planted deep enough.
	The pond floor contains too many nutrients.
	Too much shade.
	The pond is too small.
Holes are seen in water-lily leaves.	*Nymphula nymphaeata* or similar (see illustration top left).
In the spring, dead creatures (fish, frogs, newts) are seen floating in the pond.	Pond too shallow and frozen right down to the bottom.
	Insufficient oxygen supply for pond creatures during the winter months.
Pond creatures are being caught and eaten by cats.	Too little cover or refuge for pond creatures.
	Incorrect design of the edge of the pond.
The water is cloudy, green or smells rotten.	Soil too rich; fish food or organic matter in the pond is causing an excess of nutrients which, in turn, is leading to increased growth of algae.
Amphibians are spawning but no young ones are moving on to land.	Lack of plants needed for spawning.
	Fish are eating spawn and larvae.
Larger, unattractive plant containers are too visible.	Wrong choice of plants in containers (tall-growing plants or plants that do not grow very fast).
Some of the pond floor is sliding away. No plants can be planted in it.	The edge of the pond is too steep.

Remedy

Remove roots (check for tree roots).

Change the design of the edge of the pond: train the pond liner to stand up vertically along its edge (see p. 9).

A visible hole in the edge of the pond: pull the liner upwards, clean well and mend with liner mending kit or by gluing on another piece of liner.
Holes that are hard to see or locate will often require a complete rebuilding of the pond.

Make sure conditions for growing plants are optimal (see pp. 34–59). A marginal zone that is kept consistently moist will keep away garden slugs and snails.

Change the design of the edge of the pond (p. 9) or use species of plants that can cope with dryness.

Plant the water-lily in a deeper position.

Reduce the supply of nutrients (see pp. 20–26).

Make sure there is sufficient light (p. 23).

Reduce large colonies of water-lilies by division of rhizomes (p. 23).

Collect caterpillar cocoons by hand and remove eaten water-lily leaves.

A frog island.

Freezing through to the bottom can only be avoided if the water is deep enough. Steep banks will ensure sufficient depth (see The deep water zone, p. 7).

Reduce nutrient supply (see pp. 20–26). A pond with few nutrients will allow more oxygen to circulate. If necessary, reduce fish stock or overwinter fish in an aquarium in a light cellar. Plant sufficient underwater plants. They will produce oxygen until well into the autumn and even under a thin layer of ice.

Dense clumps of underwater plants offer fish hiding places. Provide a safe place for frogs, inaccessible to cats, by using island containers (illustration top right).

Allow plants to grow over the surface of the water in one part of the pond to protect pond creatures from cats, dogs and birds. A broad marshy area will prove an uncomfortably damp place for cats who like to go fishing.

During the autumn, remove certain clumps of plants in order to reduce nutrients. Install underwater plants to prevent the growth of algae. Fish out dead leaves in the autumn. Keep the fish stock low in numbers so that no extra feeding is required.

Plant underwater plants and reeds (illustration bottom right).

Lots of plant growth underwater will provide refuge for larvae. Do not place fish in a pond until it has had time to become established (*Leucaspius delineatus* and bitterlings will eat less spawn).

Plant species that remain submerged and grow far into the water along the edge of the containers. Even free-floating plants will cover the edge of the container, e.g. water soldier (see p. 56).

Install verge matting with planting pockets (illustration bottom left). Build a drystone wall (see p. 8).

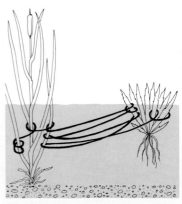

Toad spawn.

Propagating

A large number of pond plants can be propagated without any significant problems. In most cases, the simplest method is to divide the rhizome or rootstock. If a plant does not thrive, however, or if dividing it involves too much work, you may be able to propagate the plant from seed, depending on whether it is suitable for this method (see pp. 34–59). Some plants also form long shoots from which daughter plants develop.

Propagating from shoots
(illustration 1)
For propagating purposes, cut off the underwater shoot with a sharp knife or secateurs, but only cut off shoots that have already formed their own roots.

Division of rhizomes
(illustration 2)
In the autumn or spring, remove the plant – a water-lily for example – from the pond so that a rhizome can be divided. During this procedure ensure that the rhizome is not damaged and try to obtain as many roots as possible. You will only be able to divide the plant if the rhizome has formed lateral branching rhizomes (daughter plants) with their own roots.

Cut off the daughter rhizome with a sharp knife, ensuring that the cut surface is as small as possible and no stump is left on the mother plant, which might begin to decay. The wound surfaces should be dusted with charcoal powder to prevent infestation with decay-promoting bacteria.

Very robust plants with branching rhizomes (reeds, for example) cannot be taken completely out of the pond. In such cases, expose only one end of a rhizome and cut it off with scissors in such a way that it has as many roots as possible. Cover up the cut end with matter from the pond floor. The newly acquired young plant can now be planted in the desired position (see p. 19).

Dividing the rootstock
(illustration 3)
Pond plants with a well-developed rootstock (e.g. species of marsh grasses and marsh marigold) can be propagated by dividing the root-stock. Take the plant out of the pond in the autumn or spring and use a long, sharp knife to cut the rootstock into two, equal-sized parts. In the case of marsh grasses, the rootstock is often so well developed that it is recommended simply to chop it in half with a spade. The nutrient supply to above-ground parts of the plant will be somewhat limited by this

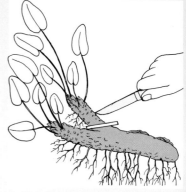

2. Use a sharp knife to divide the rhizome.

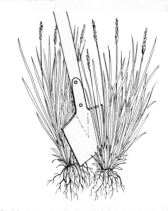

3. Use a spade to divide vigorous rootstocks, e.g. of grasses.

damage to the root. Make sure that all the outer leaves of the plant, as well as any bent, crumpled or damaged leaves, are cut off.

1. Rooted shoots can be cut off the mother plant.

Propagating from seed

Propagating from seed is time-consuming but with some plants the effort is well worthwhile (see pp. 34–59 for details of how to propagate individual plants). Use this manner of propagation only with plants whose seeds are easy to harvest, which are problem-free in respect of germination and which grow easily, such as some iris species. You can work only with pure species, not with hybrids.

Propagating from iris seeds

It is worth sowing seeds of *Iris sibirica* and *Iris pseudacorus* as, with correct care, they will produce many, easily isolated, individual plantlets. Like many other northern European marginal plants, the iris is a cold-germinator and requires low temperatures for germination.

Seed harvest

(illustration 4)

Do not remove the seed capsules until they are dry and brown. Simply break open the capsules with your fingers and shake out the seeds on to a piece of paper. They should be kept in a cool, dry place.

Preparing and sowing the seed

(illustration 5)

Around the middle of the second month of winter, the seed should be prepared for sowing out. Sprinkle them in a shallow dish that has been lined with damp blotting paper or kitchen towel and then stand the dish in a refrigerator. Keep the blotting paper or kitchen towel slightly moist. After about two weeks you can take the dish out of the refrigerator and remove the seeds and paper. Pack loose compost in the dish. Distribute the seeds on the compost and cover them with a very thin layer of compost. Moisten the compost well without making it waterlogged.

4. Break open a capsule and shake out the seeds.

Stand the dish on a windowsill at room temperature and make sure that the compost is kept damp. After about two weeks, the first small iris plants will appear, looking rather like grass at first glance.

Pricking out

(illustration 6)

When this miniature "lawn" has grown to about 5 cm (2 in) tall, you should prick the plantlets out into individual pots. Turn the dish upside down and carefully lift out the tangled mat of roots. Separate the mat with your fingers very carefully,

5. Stand the seeds of cold-germinating plants in a refrigerator.

to prevent damage to the roots. Gently pick the plantlets apart and plant every three or four of them in pots containing loose, nutrient-rich soil. The plantlets should be placed in a sunny window for optimal growth. Make sure the compost is never allowed to dry out. When the plants are about 20 cm (8 in) high, they can be planted out in the marginal zone from about the second month of spring onwards (see p. 44).

6. Once the plantlets are about 5 cm/2 in tall, carefully pull them apart and plant three to four plants per pot.

Natural setting

Unfortunately, such a scene is rarely to be found in the wild any longer – splendid stands of common flag (Iris pseudacorus) and water-lilies (Nymphaea alba). Both species are now strictly protected. Irises and water-lilies are among the most popular pond plants, and an overwhelming selection is available in the gardening trade. Only native species should be planted in a wild pond but any cultivars will suit an ornamental pond.

Emerging dragonflies

To encourage dragonflies the pond will require a marginal zone thickly planted with reeds and rushes so that the larvae can climb out of the water shortly before emerging from the chrysalis.

A selection of plants for a garden pond

The available range of pond plants is both varied and enticingly beautiful. To help you to choose the right plants for your pond, we have compiled a selection of the most beautiful and popular plants.

Plants for wild and ornamental ponds

The right choice of pond plants will depend first of all on the type of pond you have decided to make. A wild pond should create the right conditions for many native plant and animal species. Only native plants that are obtainable from the gardening trade should be used for such a pond.

You can plant any plant species from the gardening trade (even cultivars) in an ornamental pond.

Explanation of keywords

The following pages will give you detailed instructions for care with information on:

Name: The first name given is the botanical name, followed by the common one.

Natural occurrence: States the natural habitat of the plant.

Flower: Details about flowering time, colours and appearance of the flowers.

Growth: Lifespan of the plant (annual or perennial), appearance, height in a garden pond.

Position: Information about the correct zone required in the pond,

depth of water and optimal conditions of light for the plant. Advice will also be given on whether the plant is suitable for planting in a running stream.

Planting: Indication as to spacing/density (number of plants per m²), compost and planting tips. It is assumed that you are stocking a well-cared-for pond containing nutrient-poor, almost neutral (pH factor around 7) floor matter or planting compost (see p. 20). If the plant has special requirements with respect to nutrient content or acidity, you will be advised what to do to create this.

NB: You can check the nutrient content and pH factor yourself.

● Flourishing underwater plants and algae are a sign that the nutrient content of the pond water is too high. Fast-growing marginal plants show that the nutrient content is too high in the pond floor. In these cases, you can reduce the amount of nutrients by adopting certain measures of care (see pp. 20–27).

● Dip a pH indicator strip in a glass of pond water (pond water and floor have about the same

acidity value). Read the pH value from the colour scale. As a rule, it should be almost neutral (around 7). If the pH value differs greatly from the medium range, help is needed for plants that prefer neutral soil (all plants on the following pages that do not mention the need for special requirements). This means that if the pH value is below 5, you should add a handful of lime to the roots (not caustic lime). If the pH value is over 8, add a handful of well-rotted bark mulch to the roots. You can also buy pond compost with varying pH factors in the gardening trade.

Care: Tells you the most important measures of care and whether the plant is hardy.

Propagation: The most successful propagating method is described.

Special feature: Special point of interest about the plant.

My tip: Advice and tips from the author's personal experience and information on whether the plant will flourish in a shady position.

Warning: This keyword will indicate whether the plant is toxic or contains skin-irritating substances.

The symbols

	The plant will flourish in a sunny position.
	The plant prefers a semi-shady position.
	The plant will cope with, or likes, shade.
	This species is protected in the wild but available in the gardening trade.
	The plant is toxic.

Flowering rush, reedmace, Pontederia cordata and purple loosestrife are popular plants for a marginal zone.

A sea of flowers and greenery

Marginal plants

The marginal zone is the decorative frame of any garden pond. A rich variety of species and a colourful profusion of flowers should abound. Make as much space as possible for this zone in your garden pond.

Splendid flowers, unusually-shaped leaves and delicate grasses are all excellent marginal plants. All of them require damp or wet soil for their proper development. When growing naturally in the wild, the roots or upperparts of shoots of marginal plants remain immersed in water. This zone in your garden pond can be full of flowers from spring to autumn if you choose the right species of plants. The most varied species of insect are also at home here which, in turn, will attract songbirds, frogs, toads and newts.

The piston-shaped inflorescence of sweet flag.

The flowers of water plantain open in the afternoon.

Acorus calamus
sweet flag

Sweet flag, which originates from Asia, is a healing plant. Its rhizomes contain etheric oils that were once used for medicinal purposes in ancient Egypt.

Natural occurrence: In reed thickets of still or slow-flowing waters; on muddy ground.

Flower: Late spring to mid-summer. Inconspicuous, greenish, clumped together in a spadix.

Growth: Perennial with fast-growing rhizome. It will grow slowly in a newly built, nutrient-poor pond, later more vigorously. Height 50–120 cm (20–48 in).

Position: Marginal zone. Depth of water 0–10 cm (0–4 in). Sun or semi-shade.

Planting: 1 per m²; in pond floor or container. Add a handful of garden soil to the rhizome.

Care: Divide the rhizome if it proliferates fast. The plant does not need to be cut back but, if desired, cut back in spring. Hardy.

Propagation: Division of rhizome.

Warning: Contains substances that irritate the skin and mucous membranes.

Alisma plantago-aquatica
water plantain

Natural occurrence: Among the reeds of still or slow-flowing waters; on nutrient-rich, muddy ground.

Flower: All summer. Small, white panicle approximately 20–40 cm (8–16 in) tall.

Growth: Perennial; forms dense clumps. Height 20–90 cm (8–36 in).

Position: Marginal and shallow water zones, also in streams. Depth of water 0–30 cm (0–12 in). Sun and semi-shade.

Planting: 2 per m²; pond floor or container. Young plants should not be planted underwater.

Care: In spring remove old stalks and leaves. If it grows too vigorously, cut off inflorescences before the seeds are ripe. Hardy.

Propagation: Division of rootstock. Also self-sowing, then prick out young plants.

My tip: Suitable for a marginal zone with great fluctuations in water levels.

Warning: This plant is toxic.

Trifid bur-marigold flowers until the first frosts.

Flowering rush grows well among reeds.

Bidens tripartita
trifid bur-marigold

This plant has two sharply indented bristles or burs on its seeds, which cling to the coats of passing animals and help to disperse the seeds.

Natural occurrence: On the edges of ponds and ditches; in nutrient-rich soils.

Flower: Mid-summer to mid-autumn. Inconspicuous, small, single, yellow-brown composite flowers.

Growth: Annual; forms a dense clump. Height 15–120 cm (6–48 in).

Position: Marginal zone and damp edge of pond. Depth of water up to 10 cm (4 in). Sunny.

Planting: 3 per m²; pond floor.

Care: Allow plants to form seeds and remove dead parts of plants in spring. If cut back too soon, the plant will disappear from the pond. If it increases too much, cut off the greater proportion of seeds before they ripen.

Propagation: Allow to self-sow or collect the seeds in the autumn and sow out in the last month of winter.

My tip: Suitable for a marginal zone with greatly fluctuating water levels.

Butomus umbellatus
flowering rush

The flowering rush is an attractive marginal plant. With its delicate pink flowers, it complements flowerless clumps of reeds in a garden pond.

Natural occurrence: Along banks with greatly fluctuating water levels; along still or slow-flowing waters; on humus-rich, nutrient-rich, muddy ground.

Flower: All summer. White-pink, on umbel-like inflorescences.

Growth: Perennial, with a fast-growing rhizome.

The grass-like leaves are arranged in basal rosettes, with the flower stalk growing out of the centre. Height to 120 cm (48 in).

Position: Marginal zone, also in streams. Depth of water 0–10 cm (0–4 in). Sun or shade.

Planting: 5 per m²; pond floor. Add a handful of garden soil to the roots.

Care: Cut back if the growth is too vigorous. Hardy.

Propagation: Division of rhizome or from seed.

My tip: Will thrive in a shady pond and in a marginal zone with water level fluctuations. Goes well with rushes, reed-mace and sweet flag.

Bog arum flourishes in semi-shade.

A white marsh marigold – Caltha palustris 'Alba'.

Calla palustris
bog arum

This plant was once used as a healing plant for snake bites because of its snakelike growth.
Natural occurrence: On the banks of still water, in marshy woodland; on nutrient-poor soils lacking lime.
Flower: Late spring to mid-summer. Inconspicuous, in a spadix. White spathe.
Growth: Perennial, with a rhizome. Forms dense, ground-covering clumps. Height to about 40 cm (16 in).

Position: Edges of marginal zone and damp edges of ponds, also streams. Roots only should stand in wet soil. Sun and shade.
Planting: 2 per m²; pond floor. Add a handful of well-rotted bark mulch.
Care: If it grows too fast, cut back rhizomes. Hardy.
Propagation: Division of rhizome.
My tip: Well suited to planting at the edge of shady ponds.
Warning: The toxic red berries are tempting to small children!

Caltha palustris
marsh marigold

Several different cultivars are available in the gardening trade.
Natural occurrence: On the banks of streams and ponds, along slow-flowing water, in woodlands beside meadows and watermeadows; on nutrient-rich soils.
Flower: Mid-spring to early summer. Up to 5 cm (2 in), glowing yellow.
Growth: Perennial, forms cushions. Height 30 cm (12 in).
Position: Marginal zone, also streams. Depth of water 0–5 cm (0–2 in). Sun and shade.
Planting: 2 per m²; pond floor, hanging boxes or containers. Add a handful of garden soil to the roots. Do not plant young plants underwater.
Care: Thin out flourishing neighbouring plants. If necessary, limit the expansion of plants by dividing the rootstock. Hardy.
Propagation: Division of rootstock or from seed. If it is free-standing, it will be self-sowing.
My tip: Will thrive in a shady pond.
Warning: This plant is toxic.

Marsh marigolds.

Flowering heads of the cyperus sedge.

The fluffy white seeds of cotton grass.

Carex pseudocyperus
cyperus sedge

This plant belongs to the large family of *Cyperaceae*. The genus *Carex* is the one containing the most species of the family.

Natural occurrence: In large stands of sedges on the banks of still waters, in marshy alder stands, on humus-rich, nutrient-rich, slightly acid soils. Prefers a mild climate.

Flower: Early summer. Greenish, inconspicuous flowerheads, hanging from long, thin stalks.

Growth: Perennial, tuft-forming, three-edged stalks. Height 40–90 cm (16–36 in).

Position: Marginal zone. Depth of water 0–10 cm (0–4 in). Semi-shade and shade.

Planting: 2 per m²; pond floor. Add a handful of well-rotted bark mulch.

Care: Cut off and remove bent stalks. Hardy.

Propagation: Division of rootstock.

My tip: Attractive plant for a shaded pond.

Eriophorum spp.
cotton grass

Two northern European cotton grass species are available: the broad-leaved *Eriophorum latifolium* and the narrow-leaved *E. angustifolium*. They are mainly distinguishable by their requirements with respect to the acidity of the pond floor. A soil containing lime is good for *E. latifolium*, and lime-poor soil for the narrow-leaved *E. angustifolium*.

Natural occurrence: In marshes and marshy soil around natural springs; on nutrient-poor soils.

Flower: Mid- to late spring. Inconspicuous, grass-like, on hanging flowerheads. Seeds in early to mid-summer, with pretty white, woolly tufts.

Growth: Perennial, tuft-forming. Height 20–50 cm (8–20 in).

Position: Marshy zone. Depth of water 0–5 cm (0–2 in). Sunny.

Planting: 3 per m²; pond floor. Add well-rotted bark mulch to *E. angustifolium*.

Care: Fast-growing neighbouring plants should be thinned out when necessary. Hardy.

Propagation: Divide rootstock.

Equisetum fluviatile
water horsetail

Natural occurrence:
Along still or slow-flowing
waters; on muddy soil
with few nutrients.
Flower: None. Propagation
from spores that are
formed on inconspicuous
spring shoots.
Growth: Has a perennial
basic axil that creeps
through the mud, from
which 30–120 cm
(12–48 in) tall shoots
grow up. The leaves have
regressed to small scales
attached to the knot
points along the stalk.
Position: Marginal zone.
Depth of water about
5 cm (2 in). Sunny.
Planting: 5 per m²; in
pond floor or container.
Care: Avoid shade
created by taller-growing,
neighbouring plants.
Hardy.
Propagation: Division of
the branching, creeping
basic axil.
Special feature: The
ancestors of the present-
day horsetail were
instrumental in the build-
up of forests during the
carboniferous era of
Earth's history when
the coal seams were
being laid down.
Warning: This plant
is toxic.

Water horsetail requires a very sunny position.

Hemp agrimony is a favourite haunt of butterflies.

Meadowsweet flowers smell of vanilla and almonds.

Eupatorium cannabinum
hemp agrimony

Hemp agrimony is ideal for planting an area of the pond intended as a refuge for pond creatures. Its luxuriant inflorescences are a favourite haunt of many butterfly species.
Natural occurrence: In clearings, edges of woodland and banks; on moist, humus-rich soils with plenty of nutrients and lime.
Flower: Mid-summer to early autumn. Dark red to reddish-violet, with umbel-like inflorescences.

Growth: Perennial shrub with tripartite, partly reddish leaves. Height 75–150 cm (30–60 in).
Position: Edge of marginal zones, moist and dry edges of ponds. The best position is the northern edge of the pond as it will tend to overshadow other plants. Only the roots should be allowed to stand in wet soil. Sun or semi-shade.
Planting: 3 per m²; pond floor. Add a handful of garden soil and a little lime to the roots.
Care: Cut off any dead stalks in the spring. Hardy.
Propagation: Division of rootstock.

Filipendula ulmaria
meadowsweet

Meadowsweet belongs among the *Rosaceae*. Its flowers have a scent reminiscent of vanilla and almonds and will attract a variety of different insects.
Natural occurrence: In water meadows, along ditches and woodland near meadows; on nutrient-rich soils.
Flower: All summer. A panicle with many small white flowers.
Growth: Perennial shrub with feathery leaves. Height 50–150 cm (20–60 in).

Position: Outer edge of marginal zone and moist edge of pond. Depth of water 0–3 cm (0–1¼ in). Sun or semi-shade.
Planting: 2 per m²; pond floor. Add a handful of garden soil to the roots.
Care: Cut back old stalks in the spring. Hardy.
Propagation: Divide rootstock.

Marsh gentians are delicate, sun-loving beauties.

Mare's tail will create a miniature "forest of firs".

Gentiana pneumo-nanthe
marsh gentian

 P

In the wild, marsh gentian is able to compete with other plants only on very nutrient-poor soil.

Natural occurrence: In marshy meadows with peaty, humus-rich soils that are poor in nutrients or lime.

Flower: Mid-summer to mid-autumn. Bell-shaped, 2–3 cm ($^3/_4$–1$^1/_4$ in), blue flowers – several to a stalk.

Growth: Perennial. Narrow, lancet-shaped leaves. Height 15–40 cm (6–16 in).

Position: Outer edge of marginal zone. Only the roots should be allowed to stand in wet soil. Very sunny site needed.

Planting: 3 per m²; pond floor or hanging boxes. It can only survive in garden ponds if the soil is nutri-ent-rich. Add a handful of garden soil to the roots. Make sure that it receives plenty of sunlight.

Care: If the plant does not thrive, add fresh garden soil to the roots. Avoid shade and regularly thin out neighbouring plants. Hardy.

Propagation: Divide root-stock.

Hippuris vulgaris
mare's tail

This plant has leaves like soft conifer needles which are arranged in spirals along the stem like the tiny branches of a fir tree.

Natural occurrence: In clear, cool waters; on humus-rich, nutrient-poor soils.

Flower: All summer. Inconspicuous, green, arranged singly in leaf axils that are above the surface of the water.

Growth: Perennial. Forms dense clumps. Height 20–30 cm (8–12 in) above the surface of the water.

Position: Marshy zone, also along streams. Depth of water 5–20 cm (2–8 in). Sun and shade.

Planting: 5 per m² ; pond floor. Young plants can be planted in water that is 10 cm (4 in) deep. When planting, make sure you note the transition from underwater leaves (soft, broad) to above-water leaves (needle-like, firm).

Care: Cut back if the plant proliferates excessively in undesirable areas. Hardy.

Propagation: Cut off shoots and replant them elsewhere.

My tip: Suitable for a shady pond and for disguising the edges of containers.

Iris pseudacorus gives a splendid display of flowers.

Iris sibirica has lovely blue and white flowers.

Iris pseudacorus
common flag

Common flag is characterised by its stiff, sword-like leaves.
Natural occurrence: In marshy meadows, woodland along marshland, near reeds, along ditches; on nutrient-rich soils that are usually covered in water.
Flower: Late spring to early summer. Several large, yellow flowers on one stalk.
Growth: Perennial. With a rhizome. Sword-shaped leaves. Height to 80–100 cm (32–40 in).

Position: Marginal zone, also streams. Depth of water 0–10 cm (0–4 in). Sun and semi-shade.
Planting: 3 per m²; pond floor. Add a handful of garden soil to the roots.
Care: During the spring, cut off old stalks that have tipped over into the water. Make sure that smaller, light-loving neighbouring plants are not swamped by the irises. Hardy.
Propagation: Division of rhizome or from seed (see p. 31).
My tip: Will also thrive in a shady pond but will then form fewer flowers.
Warning: This plant is toxic.

Iris sibirica

Various cultivated varieties are obtainable in the gardening trade but are not always easy to come by, e.g. 'Maggie Lee' (light, reddish-violet), 'Snow Bounty' (white) and 'Tropic Night' (deep velvety bluish-purple).
Natural occurrence: In marshy meadows; on nutrient-poor soils containing lime. Rare.
Flower: Early summer. Blue and white with dark blue veins.
Growth: Perennial. Narrow leaves that lie close to the

stalk. Young plants look grass-like. Height 60–80 cm (24–32 in).
Position: Marginal zone, also along streams. Depth of water 0–5 cm (0–2 in). Sunny.
Planting: 3 per m²; pond floor, container or hanging box. Add a handful of garden soil and a little lime to the roots.
Care: Watch out for young plants as they are easily confused with grass and weeded out. Do not cut older plants until spring. Hardy.
Propagation: Division of rhizome. Propagation from seed in pure species (see p. 31).

Iris laevigata

This is a Japanese relative of the northern European yellow and blue irises. It will not thrive amid northern European flora, so should only be planted in ornamental ponds.

Natural occurrence: In marshy meadows in eastern Siberia, Korea, Japan and China; on humus-rich, nutrient-rich soils.

Flower: Early to mid-summer. Dark blue with yellow central stripe on the pendulous petals. Cultivars are: 'Alba' (pure white, with blue-red spotted, pendulous petals), 'Atropurpurea' (violet, purple red or blue), 'Niagara' (ice blue, double), 'Regal' (purple red, very large), 'Variegata' (light blue).

Growth: Perennial. With a rhizome. Smooth leaves without a central rib. Height 60–80 cm (24–32 in).

Position: Marginal zone. Depth of water, about 15 cm (6 in). Sunny.

Planting: 3 per m²; pond floor. Add a handful of garden soil to the roots.

Care: Cut off leaves that are bent over in the water, and cut off stalks in spring. Hardy.

Propagation: Division of rhizome. Propagation from seed is not possible for hybrid varieties.

Iris ensata
bog iris

This iris thrives only in ornamental ponds.

Natural occurrence: In damp meadows in Japan, Manchuria, Korea and China; on humus-rich, lime-free, nutrient-rich soils.

Flower: Early to mid-summer. The original species is purple red with broad, pendulous petals and narrow dome petals. There are attractive cultivars (photos 1–4, below right).

Growth: Perennial. Leaves with central rib. Height 60–80 cm (24–32 in).

Position: Marginal zone. Depth of water 0–5 cm (0–2 in). Sunny.

Planting: The ideal situation is when the rootstock of the plant is covered in water during the spring and is dry during the summer (edge of pond). Leaves that have bent over into the water should be cut off; cut back stalks in the spring. Hardy.

Propagation: see *Iris laevigata*.

A selection of particularly colourful varieties
1. 'Embosed'
2. 'Herwig'
3. 'Wella'
4. 'Good Omen'

Iris laevigata has a yellow central stripe.

Creeping Jenny is ideal for the edge of the pond.

Purple loosestrife inflorescences are 10 cm (4 in) long.

Lysimachia nummularia
creeping Jenny

Natural occurrence: In meadows, along ditches, banks and water meadows; on nutrient-rich soils.

Flower: Late spring to mid-summer. Yellow, about 1.5 cm (½ in) tall, single flowers in leaf axils.

Growth: Perennial, with a prostrate stalk, forms dense clumps. Height about 10 cm (4 in).

Position: Marginal zone and pond edge, also stream bed. Depth of water 0–10 cm (0–4 in). Sun and shade.

Planting: 5 per m²; pond floor, hanging boxes or containers. Add a handful of garden soil to the roots. Young plants can also be planted under-water.

Care: Avoid smothering by other plants. Hardy.

Propagation: Cut off rooted lateral shoots.

My tip: This plant is particularly suitable for groundcover along the edge of a pond and for disguising the edges of containers. Will thrive in a shady pond.

Lythrum salicaria
purple loosestrife

A striking, late-flowering marginal plant with purple red inflorescences.

Natural occurrence: In water meadows, along banks and ditches; on nutrient-rich soil with very little lime.

Flower: Early summer to early autumn. Small, purple red, candle-shaped inflorescences.

Growth: Perennial, vigorous shrub. The lower part of the plant tends to be woody. Height is approximately 50–120 cm (20–48 in).

Position: Marshy zone. Depth of water 0–15 cm (0–6 in). Sun and semi-shade.

Planting: 2 per m²; pond floor or container. Add a handful of garden soil to the roots. The young plants should not be entirely covered with water.

Care: Do not cut old stalks until spring so that the plant can form ripe seed and self-sow. It provides favourite winter quarters for pond creatures. Thin out rampant neighbouring plants. Hardy.

Propagation: Division of rootstock or from seed. This plant has light-germinating seed. Place the seed in a bright position and keep moist.

Bogbean has white and pink, fringed petals.

Reeds can grow up to 2 m (80 in) tall.

Menyanthes trifoliata
bogbean

 P

Used in the past to reduce a fever.
Natural occurrence: In flat marshes and marshes around natural springs, dried up parts of marshy lakes; on humus-contain-ing, nutrient-poor soils.
Flower: Late spring to early summer. Inflorescence of single, white, fringed flowers with a delicate tinge of pink.
Growth: Perennial, with a rhizome, does not form very dense clumps. Clover-like leaves. Height to 35 cm (14 in).

Position: Marginal zone, also in streams. Depth of water to 10 cm (4 in). Sunny.
Planting: 5 per m²; pond floor. Plant young plants in such a way that the greater part of the plant is protruding from the water.
Care: Cut back any fast-growing neighbouring plants. Hardy.
Propagation: Divide the rooted, creeping stalk. Also possible from seed, but difficult.
Special feature: Large insects, like bumble bees, are necessary for pollination. The plant has created a device for keeping away smaller insects by developing fringes on its petals.

Phragmites australis
common reed

With their dense, tall growth, reeds offer a habitat to many creatures.
Natural occurrence: Along still or slow-flowing waters, in marshy meadows or marshy alder clumps; on nutrient-rich soils.
Flower: Mid-summer to early autumn. Green to reddish panicles.
Growth: Perennial, with fast-growing rhizomes, forms dense stands. Height up to 2 m (80 in).
Position: Marginal and shallow water zones, also

moist edge of pond. Depth of water 0–30 cm (0–12 in). Sun and shade.
Planting: 5 per m²; pond floor or container. Nutrient-poor compost helps to check the speed of growth of this vigorous plant. When planting, make sure that small, light-loving plants are not overshadowed.
Care: Cut back old stalks in early spring. Hardy.
Propagation: Division of rhizome.
My tip: Reeds can form an attractive border along the northern edge of the pond because of their height. Will thrive along a shaded pond.

Pontederia cordata flowers until the first frost.

Greater spearwort is an evergreen pond plant.

Pontederia cordata

This plant, which originates from North America, is suitable only in an ornamental pond in Britain and Europe.
Natural occurrence: Along still or slow-moving waters; on nutrient-rich soils.
Flower: From early summer until the first frosts. Small, blue, white or pink on a head about 10 cm (4 in) long.
Growth: Perennial, with fast-growing rhizome. Large, soft, shiny leaves. Height 50cm (20 in).

Position: Marginal zone, also in streams. Depth of water up to 20 cm (8 in). Sun and semi-shade.
Planting: 3 per m²; pond floor. This nutrient-loving plant should be planted only in nutrient-poor compost to prevent it from crowding out other species.
Care: Occasionally thin out. Cut off above-ground parts of the plant in the autumn. Protect the root-stock in winter with a covering of dead leaves.
Propagation: Division of rhizome or sowing out from early to mid-spring. Allow seed to germinate at 12–15°C (54–59°F), then keep cool and plant out in late spring.

Ranunculus lingua
greater spearwort

    P

The name is derived from its spear-shaped under-water leaves.
Natural occurrence: In the reeds along still or slow-flowing water; on nutrient-poor soils that contain a little lime and are sometimes flooded. Rare.
Flower: All summer. 2–4 cm (³/₄–1¹/₂ in) tall, yellow single flowers on the ends of stalks.
Growth: Perennial, with fast-growing rhizome. Narrow, deep green, firm leaves above water; soft,

light brown underwater leaves. Height 100–150 cm (40–60 in).
Position: Marginal and shallow water zones. Depth of water 0–40 cm (0–16 in). Sun and semi-shade.
Planting: 3 per m²; pond floor or container.
Care: In the spring, cut off parts of plants that are growing into the middle of smaller ponds. Hardy.
Propagation: Cut off rooted parts of rhizomes and replant.
My tip: Suitable for marginal zone with great fluctuations in water levels.
Warning: This plant is toxic.

The leaves of arrowhead point north and south.

Branched bur-reed.

Sagittaria sagittifolia
arrowhead

Arrowhead has large leaves shaped like the barbs of arrows.
Natural occurrence: In reeds along slow-flowing waters, along ditches; on humus-containing, nutrient-rich, sandy or muddy soils. Rare.
Flower: All summer. About 2 cm (³/₄ in) tall, white with a red spot in the centre, in vertically consecutive whorls.
Growth: Perennial tubers, arrow-shaped leaves. Height 20–100 cm (8–40 in).

Position: Marginal zone, also along streams. Depth of water 0–20 cm (0–8 in). Sun and shade.
Planting: 2 per m²; pond floor or container. In the case of young plants, above-surface leaves should not end up underwater.
Care: Thin out dense growth. Remove dead stalks in the spring. Hardy.
Propagation: Remove tubers from shoot ends in the autumn and replant.
My tip: Will thrive in a shady pond.
Warning: Tubers may cause skin irritation.

Sparganium erectum
branched bur-reed

Branched bur-reed is a very undemanding marginal plant. Its seedhead resembles a curled-up hedgehog.
Natural occurrence: In reed thickets along banks of still or slow-flowing waters; on nutrient-rich and lime-rich soils.
Flower: Mid-summer to early autumn. Inconspicuous, spherical flowerheads.
Growth: Perennial. The rhizome of one single plant may form a dense thicket in just a few years.

Height to approximately 50 cm (20 in).
Position: Marginal zone. Depth of water 0–25 cm (0–10 in). Sun and semi-shade.
Planting: 2 per m²; pond floor. Make sure that lower-growing plants are not overshadowed.
Care: Cut off old leaves during the spring. Hardy.
Propagation: Division of rhizome or from seed.
Special feature: This plant stores oxalate crystals in its leaves to protect it from being eaten by grazing animals.

49

Typha spp.
reedmace

There are several species of reedmace. In addition to the narrow-leaved *Typha angustifolia* there is the small *Typha minima* and the broad-leaved reedmace (*Typha latifolia*), all of which are suitable for garden ponds.

Natural occurrence: Among the reeds in still, warm waters; on nutrient-poor, muddy ground with little lime. Rare.

Flower: All summer. Very small, greenish, arranged in large bulrush-like inflorescences. Height 1–2 m (40–80 in).

Position: Marginal and shallow water zones. Depth of water to 20 cm (8 in). Sun and semi-shade.

Planting: 3 per m²; pond floor or container. Not on the south side of the pond as it would overshadow other plants.

Care: In spring, cut off old stalks above the surface of the water. Hardy.

Propagation: Division of rhizome.

My tip: The small reedmace only grows to a height of 70 cm (28 in) and is, therefore, well suited to planting in small ponds.

Narrow-leaved reedmace is very suitable for larger ponds.

With their many colourful varieties and cultivars, water-lilies are the queens of the pond.

A carpet of colour over the pond

Floating and surface plants

Splendid surface plants such as the colourful water-lilies and other, less well-known plants, give a garden pond its real charm.

Floating plants usually have no roots anchored in the pond floor; instead, they tend to float on the surface of the water. The splendid water-lilies are the most sought-after surface plants but there are others that are just as attractive. These offer a useful alternative to water-lilies as they will also thrive in small ponds.

Do not plant too many surface plants. It is better to have one plant that flourishes than too many that are set too close together and entirely cover the surface of the water, cutting off light from underwater plants.

Water starwort forms pretty leaf rosettes.

The spherical flowers of the yellow water-lily.

Callitriche palustris
water starwort

Water starwort is an amphibious plant. It can grow as a water plant or as a land plant, depending on its position.

Natural occurrence: In shallow, still waters; on humus-rich, nutrient-poor, muddy soils with little lime. Rare.

Flower: Late spring to mid-autumn. Inconspicuous underwater flowers.

Growth: Perennial; forms small leafy rosettes which either float on the surface of the water or root in damp soil. Protrudes about 5 cm (2 in) from the water.

Position: Marginal and shallow water zone. Depth of water about 0–60 cm (0–24 in). Sun and semi-shade.

Planting: 5 per m²; pond floor. Plant in the shallow water zone so that the leaf rosettes float on top of the water.

Care: Prevent excessive growth of underwater plants and cloudy water caused by algae. Hardy.

Propagation: Cut off rooted lateral shoots and replant.

Special feature: Will stay green in winter and supply the pond with oxygen.

Nuphar lutea
yellow water-lily

    P

The yellow water-lily is a surface plant. The least yellow water-lily (*Nuphar pumila*) is similar but smaller.

Natural occurrence: In still or slow-flowing, nutrient-poor or nutrient-rich waters; on humus-rich sand or gravel soils.

Flower: All summer. Glowing yellow, spherical, on stalks that are held 10–20 cm (4–8 in) above the water.

Growth: Perennial, with rhizomes. Soft underwater leaves; large, oval, floating leaves, to 40 cm (16 in) long, on long stalks.

Position: Deep water zone. Depth of water 0.8–2 m (32–80 in). Sun and semi-shade.

Planting: 1 per m²; pond floor. Add a handful of garden soil to the roots.

Care: Keep free of underwater plants. It will not thrive in cloudy water. If it grows excessively, cut off some floating leaves close to the rhizome. Hardy.

Propagation: Division of rhizome.

My tip: Also suitable for small, shallow ponds.

Warning: This plant is toxic.

Water fringe thrives in regions with mild winters.

Nymphoides peltata
water fringe

  P

The water fringe, along with its closest relative, the bogbean, belongs to the family *Gentianaceae*. Being a surface plant, it is an exception among the *Gentianaceae*, which normally only occur in mountain pastures and in marshland. The seedpods are egg-shaped, 1 cm (under ¹/₂ in) long capsules which contain disc-shaped seeds. The seeds are able to float on the surface of the water and stick to the feathers of waterfowl. In this way,

they are distributed to other bodies of water.
Natural occurrence: Mostly in shallow, still or slow-flowing waters; on nutrient-rich soils. Prefers a climate with mild winters. Rare.
Flower: Mid- to late summer. Yellow, funnel-shaped, up to 7 cm (less than 3 in) long, with fringes on the petals. 2–5 flowers protrude in clusters above the surface of the water.
Growth: Perennial, water-lily-like. Small, round surface leaves do not grow from a rhizome as in the case of the water-lily, but from immersed, branching stalks. It protrudes

approximately 10 cm (4 in) above the water.
Position: Shallow and deep water zones, or along streams. Depth of water 0.5–1.5 m (20–60 in).
Planting: 2 per m²; pond floor or plant container. Add one handful of garden soil to the roots.
Care: If necessary, cut back fast-growing neighbouring plants. Make sure that the submerged stalks are not damaged. Hardy.
Propagation: Division of branching basal axis. Also from seed.
Special feature: Water fringe is an indicator of a warm climate, which means it will only grow

in the wild in regions with a mild climate.
My tip: Unlike water-lilies, water fringe will also thrive in small, fairly shallow garden ponds. If you have both plants in your pond, the very fast-growing water-lilies will have to be cut back occasionally, so that the water fringe is not crowded out.

The tropical water-lily Nymphaea stellata 'Caerulea'.

The European water-lily Nymphaea alba.

Nymphaea alba
white water-lily

   P

The white water-lily is a European surface plant. A great variety of cultivars have been raised from it.

Natural occurrence: In still, not too cloudy, waters with a depth of up to approximately 3 m (120 in); on humus-containing, nutrient-rich muddy soils.

Flower: Early summer to early autumn. 10–20 cm (4–8 in) large, white with yellow stamens. The flowers open in the morning and close again in the evening.

Growth: Perennial, with a rhizome. Roundish surface leaves with a diameter of up to 40 cm (16 in), on metre-long (3 ft) stalks, which grow from rhizome-like flower stalks.

Position: Deep water zone. Depth of water 0.7– 3 m (28–120 in). Sunny.

Planting: 1 per m²; pond floor or container (see Planting water-lilies, p. 19).

Care: With plenty of sun-light and a sufficient depth of water, it should flourish very well in a garden pond (see Care of water-lilies, p. 23). Hardy.

Propagation: Division of rhizome.

Warning: This plant is toxic.

Other species

Cultivars in many different colour variations (from yellow to red to copper-coloured) are available. Most varieties are hardy and can remain in the pond. Some varieties have been created that remain smaller and will, therefore, flourish in shallower water, e.g. *Nymphaea candida* or *Nymphaea odorata*. They are suitable for small ponds or shallow water zones.

A large number of tropical relatives is also available. The best known one is the giant Amazonian water-lily (*Victoria amazonica*) which, because of its size (leaves with a diameter of up to 2 m /80 in across), rarely finds a home in garden ponds. In tropical species, the scale of colours is even greater, ranging right through to shades of blue. Their flowers do not float on the surface but are held above the surface of the water on stalks. They are sensitive to low tempera-tures and have to be removed from the pond in early autumn and over-wintered in a warm place (see Non-hardy pond plants, p. 24).

Amphibious bistort thrives in deeper water.

Pondweed can cope with shade.

Polygonum amphibium
amphibious bistort

Depending on its position, the amphibious bistort will occur as a water or land plant. In garden ponds the water variety is usually used as a surface plant.
Natural occurrence: In colonies of water-lilies and among reeds along banks of still water; on lime-free, nutrient-rich, marshy soils.
Flower: Early summer to early autumn. Small, pink, longish heads, arranged in inflorescences protruding 10–15 cm (4–6 in) above the surface of the water.

Growth: Perennial, with a rhizome. Surface leaves up to 20 cm (8 in) long.
Position: Shallow and deep water zones, along streams. Depth of water 30–100 cm (12–40 in). Sunny and semi-shady.
Planting: 2 per m²; pond floor. Add a handful of garden soil to the roots.
Care: Cut back leaves in summer or autumn if it proliferates excessively. Hardy.
Propagation: Division of rhizome.
Warning: The leaves may cause skin irritation.

Potamogeton natans
broad-leaved
pondweed

Even though pondweed occurs only in deeper waters in the wild, this surface plant will thrive in garden ponds at only 40 cm (16 in) deep.
Natural occurrence: In still or slow-flowing waters; on nutrient-poor, marshy soils.
Flower: All summer. Green, piston-shaped inflorescences.
Growth: Perennial, prostrate rhizome, thick like a tuber, rampant growth.

Position: Deep water zone, also in streams. Depth of water from 40 cm (16 in). Sun and shade.
Planting: 3 per m²; pond floor. Small plants can be placed at the desired depth but not in ponds with very cloudy water.
Care: If the plant proliferates excessively, cut off leaf stalks close to the rhizome. Hardy.
Propagation: Division of rhizome.
My tip: Thrives in a shady pond.

Water soldier grows anywhere in a pond.

Water chestnut forms floating leaf rosettes.

Stratiotes aloides
water soldier

   P

Water soldier is a floating plant that will thrive even in very polluted water.
Natural occurrence: In still, nutrient-poor, lime-free water in positions sheltered from the wind.
Flower: Late spring to mid-summer. White petals, 3–4 cm (1¼–1½ in), with yellow spot in centre.
Growth: Perennial, with rhizomes, forms large carpets. Stiff, spine-edged leaves arranged in rosettes.
Position: Shallow and deep water zones. Sun and semi-shade.

Planting: 2 per m²; preferably in a position where it can hold on (e.g. beside an island container).
Care: Occasionally cut back so that it cannot take away the light from other underwater plants. To do this, pull shoots from the water and cut off about half of the length. Hardy.
Propagation: Cut off rooted shoots and replant.
Special feature: Forms roots in the autumn, with which it pulls itself down to the pond floor for overwintering.

Trapa natans
water chestnut

 P

This surface plant derives its name from the seeds, which look like pointed nuts with a hook. When the ripe seeds fall, they anchor themselves in the mud. From these buried seeds, new plants grow to the surface. The water chestnut will not grow in waters that are too cold.
Natural occurrence: In still waters in regions with a mild climate; on humus-containing, nutrient-rich marshy soils with little lime. Roots in a depth of 1–2 m (40–80 in).

Flower: Early to mid-summer. Inconspicuous, whitish, arranged in the leaf axils. The seeds ripen during early autumn.
Growth: Annual; floating rosette of small, diamond-shaped leaves on a 1–2 m (40–80 in) long stalk that is anchored in the pond floor.
Position: Shallow and deep water zones. Depth of water 40–150 cm (16–60 in). Sunny.
Planting: 2 per m²; pond floor.
Care: No particular care is required.
Propagation: Remove the seeds in the autumn and allow them to sink to the floor where you wish them to "take".

Luxuriantly flowering common bladderwort in a moorland pool.

Nutrient regulators and suppliers of oxygen

Submerged oxygenating plants

Underwater plants are the purification workers of the garden pond. They are able to function as "nutrient-traps" and "dirt collectors".

Submerged plants play an important role in the care of a pond as they supply the pond with oxygen and remove excess nutrients dissolved in the pond water, which would otherwise quickly lead to excessive proliferation of algae which can make the water cloudy. Any excess nutrients in the mud can be removed from the pond through regular thinning out of underwater plants. In addition, the underwater plants help to keep the pond clear, as floating substances land on their leaves and are "held" there. They should be included in every garden pond. A further advantage is that they provide a refuge for many small pond creatures.

Rigid hornwort.

Important underwater species.

Ceratophyllum demersum
rigid hornwort

Flower: Early summer to early autumn. Inconspicuous, small, underwater flowers.
Growth: Perennial, rootless.
Position: Shallow and deep water zones, also in streams. Depth of water up to 150 cm (60 in). Sun and shade.
Planting: 5 per m²; sink using a planting stone.
Care: Thin out if necessary. Hardy.
Propagation: Cut off lateral branching shoots and sink them.
My tip: Will thrive in a shady pond.

Chara spp.
algae
(photo 1)

Flower: None.
Growth: Perennial; many branches, forms extensive underwater mats.
Position: Shallow and deep water zones. Depth of water up to 50 cm (20 in). Sunny.
Planting: 5 per m²; sink with the help of a planting stone.
Care: Thin out if necessary. Hardy.
Propagation: Cut off branches and replant.

Myriophyllum spp.
water milfoil
(photo 2) **P**

Flower: All summer. Small, pink, on an upright head.
Growth: Perennial, delicate, strongly branching, underwater leaves.
Position: Shallow and deep water zones, also along streams. Depth of water about 1 m (40 in). Sun and shade.
Planting: 5 per m²; sink with a planting stone.
Care: Occasionally cut back neighbouring underwater plants. Hardy.
Propagation: Cut off lateral shoots and sink them.

Elodea spp.
pondweed
(photos 3 and 4)

Flower: Late spring to early autumn. Does not usually flower in the northern European climate.
Growth: Perennial, proliferating, roots in pond floor. Branching stalks that float in the water.
Position: Shallow and deep water zones, also along streams. Depth of water 1 m (40 in).
Planting: 5 per m²; sink with a planting stone.
Care: Thin out regularly. Hardy.
Propagation: Cut off lateral shoots and replant.

Hottonia palustris
water violet

Flower: Late spring to early summer. White to pink with a yellow spot in the centre.
Growth: Perennial. Protrudes 15–30 cm (6–12 in) above the water.
Position: Marginal and shallow water zones. Depth of water 5–50 cm (2–20 in). Sun or shade.
Planting: 3 per m²; pond floor, container or hanging box. Add well-rotted bark mulch.
Care: Cut back proliferating colonies along the edges. Hardy.
Propagation: Cut off rooted branches of stalks and replant.
Special feature: Remains green in winter.

Utricularia vulgaris
common
bladderwort
(photos 1 and 3)

Flower: All summer. Yellow, like a snapdragon head, protruding a few centimetres above the surface of the water.
Growth: Perennial, rootless. Leaves are soft and feathery, with numerous strands that float in the water.
Position: Shallow water zone. Depth of water about 50 cm (20 in). Sunny.
Planting: 5 per m²; sink with the help of a planting stone.
Care: Thin out plants occasionally. Hardy.

Propagation: Cut off lateral shoots and sink.
Special feature: Possesses small bladders in which it captures small water creatures (see photo 1 and Rootless survivors, p. 11).

Potamogeton densus
opposite-leaved
pondweed
(photo 2)

In addition to the opposite-leaved pondweed, other species are also suitable for the garden pond, e.g. *Potamogeton pectinatus, Potamogeton crispus.*
Flower: All summer. Small, inconspicuous heads. Rare.
Growth: Perennial, delicate, up to 30 cm (12 in) long. Small leaves, 1–2 cm (¹/₂–³/₄ in), arranged in pairs close to the stalk.
Position: Shallow water zone, also streams. Depth of water 20–50 cm (8–20 in). Sunny.
Planting: 5 per m²; sink with the help of a planting stone, not too close to surface plants.
Care: Keep free of proliferating underwater plants. Hardy.
Propagation: Cut off rooted lateral shoots and replant.
Special feature: Will remain green in mild winters.

Water violets.

Utricularia vulgaris (1,3) and Potamogeton densus (2).

Index

Figures in bold indicate illustrations.

Index

Index

Acknowledgements

Some of the garden ponds depicted in this volume were designed by garden architects: Henk Weyers, Haarlem/Netherlands (p. 15, inside back cover); Felix Viell, Düsseldorf (p. 12–13).

The publishers and photographer Friedrich Strauss would like to thank the following firm for their help: Jörg Petrowsky, Aschau-Teiche, 29348 Eschede.

The publishers and the author would also like to thank Peter Stadelmann for his help in reading through the manuscript.

Author's notes

This volume is concerned with the care of pond plants. Some of the plants described here are toxic to a greater or lesser degree. In the section containing plant descriptions (pp. 34–59) the keyword "Warning" points out any specific danger to health. Any plants known to be lethally toxic or even mildly toxic to susceptible adults or children and likely to cause considerable damage to health, have been marked with a skull and crossbones symbol. Please make absolutely sure that children and pets are not allowed to consume any plants marked with the keyword "Warning" and bearing the skull and crossbones.
Some of the plants secrete skin-irritating substances, which is also indicated for individual plants. If you suffer from contact allergies, you should definitely wear protective gloves when handling these plants. As a protective measure for yourself and others, you should secure your garden pond adequately (with a fence or protective grid), particularly if there are small children in your household or if the pond is situated in a garden that is not fenced in. We strongly recommend taking out relevant insurance on the pond. Every garden pond owner must make sure that no water – whether underground or above – is able to flow on to a neighbouring plot. Check the water lines regularly and carry out any changes of water or emptying of the pond in the correct manner.

Cover photographs
Front cover: main picture, *Nymphaea*
'Lucida'; top right, *Zantedeschia
aethiopica* 'Crowborough'; middle
right, *Typha latifolia*; bottom right,
Iris laevigata.
Inside front cover: *Iris sibirica*
Inside back cover: *Lythrum salicaria*
Back cover: a garden pond scene.

Photographic acknowledgements
Becker: inside front cover, 12/13, 21,
32/33, 35, inside back cover; Eisenbiss:
p. 39; Gröger: p. 33 bottom; Natur & Text:
p. 44 right, 58 top centre, 59 left centre;
Labhardt: p. 49 right, 56 right; Andrew
Lawson: front cover, centre, top right,
middle right, bottom right; Merehurst Ltd:
back cover; Pforr: p. 47 right, 55 right;
Reinhard: p. 25, 43 right, 46 right, 48 right,
52 right, 59 top; Scherz: p. 37 right;
Schlaback-Becker: p. 15; Schimmitat-
Angerer: p. 38 left; Strauss: p. 2 top, bottom, 3 top, 5, 13 bottom, 14, 20, 27, 34,
36 left, 37 left, 38 right, 40 left, right, 41,
42 left, right, 43 left, 44 left, 45 top, centre
left, centre right, bottom left, bottom right,
46 left, 47 left, 48 left, 49 left, 50, 51, 52
left, 53, 54 left, 55 left, 56 left, 58 left, top
right, bottom centre, bottom right, 59
centre right, bottom; Tessenow: p. 57;
TIPHO/Titz: p. 4; Wothe: p. 10, 36 right,
54 right.

This edition published 1995 by
Merehurst Limited
Ferry House, 51–57 Lacy Road,
Putney, London SW15 1PR
Reprinted 1996, 2000

© 1994 Gräfe und Unzer GmbH, Munich

ISBN 1 85391 935 7

English text copyright ©
Merehurst Limited 1994
Translated by Astrid Mick
Edited by Lesley Young
Design and typesetting by
Paul Cooper Design
Illustrations by Marlene Gemke
Printed in Hong Kong by Wing King Tong Ltd